Let's Get Cooking
ITALIAN

Over **100** flavoursome dishes

igloobooks

igloobooks

Published in 2017
by Igloo Books Ltd
Cottage Farm
Sywell
NN6 0BJ
www.igloobooks.com

Designed by Nicholas Gage
Edited by Bobby Newlyn-Jones

Food photography and recipe development
© Stockfood, The Food Media Agency
Additional imagery © iStock / Getty Images
Cover images: © iStock / Getty Images

LEO002 0417
2 4 6 8 10 9 7 5 3 1
ISBN 978-1-78670-862-5

Printed and manufactured in China

Contents

Meat and Fish Dishes

SERVES: 4 | PREP TIME: 40 MINS | COOKING TIME: 30 MINS

Parmesan Stuffed Tomatoes

8 ripe beef tomatoes
salt
1 tbsp olive oil
1 onion, peeled and finely chopped
2 cloves of garlic, finely chopped
250g / 9 oz / 1 cup minced beef
1 tbsp rosemary leaves, finely chopped
2 tbsp Parmesan, grated

1. Using a teaspoon, hollow out the tomatoes, discarding the seeds.
2. Sprinkle the insides with a little salt and leave to drain upside down for 30 minutes.
3. Meanwhile, fry the onion and garlic in the oil until translucent.
4. Add the beef and rosemary then turn up the heat and fry. Stir until the beef is cooked and then season.
5. Stir in the Parmesan and leave to cool.
6. Preheat the oven to 200°C (180° fan) / 400F / gas 6.
7. Fill the tomatoes with the beef mixture and place in a roasting tin.
8. Drizzle with olive oil and bake in the oven for 30 minutes, or until the tomatoes are soft but retaining their shape.
9. Serve hot or warm with salad.

Beef Carpaccio

250 g / 9 oz beef fillet, trimmed
handful rocket leaves
Parmesan shavings
1 tbsp capers, drained
extra virgin olive oil
½ lemon, juiced
salt and pepper

1. Place the fillet in the freezer for 30 minutes to firm it up and make it easier to slice.
2. Slice the fillet as thinly as you possibly can with a razor-sharp knife. Place film over each slice to prevent discolouring and use it to stop the slices sticking together. You can keep them this way in the refrigerator until serving.
3. 30 minutes before serving remove the beef from the refrigerator and bring up to room temperature.
4. Decorate with the rocket, Parmesan and capers and drizzle over the oil and lemon. Season and serve.

Red Pepper and Ham Tortilla

60 ml / 2 fl. oz / ¼ cup olive oil
1 onion, thinly sliced
1 red pepper, quartered and thinly sliced
6 large eggs
1 tbsp flat leaf parsley, chopped
4 slices ham, cooked
salt and pepper

1. Heat half the oil in a non-stick frying pan over a medium-low heat. Fry the onion and red pepper with a pinch of salt and pepper for 15 minutes, stirring occasionally, until soft and sweet.
2. Meanwhile, gently beat the eggs in a jug to break up the yolks. When the vegetables are ready, stir them into the eggs with the parsley and ham, then season with salt and pepper.
3. Wipe out the frying pan with a piece of kitchen paper and add the rest of the oil. Pour in the egg mixture and cook over a gentle heat for 6-8 minutes or until the egg has set around the outside, but the centre is still a bit soft.
4. Turn it out onto a plate, then slide it back into the pan and cook the other side for 4-6 minutes or until the egg is just set in the very centre.
5. Leave to cool for 5 minutes then cut into wedges and serve.

SERVES: 4 | PREP TIME: 20 MINS | COOKING TIME: 1 HOUR

Cod and Vegetable Minestrone

1 tbsp olive oil
70 g / 2 ¾ oz / ⅓ cup pancetta or
smoked streaky bacon, chopped
1 onion, peeled and finely chopped
1 carrot, peeled and finely chopped
2 celery stalks, finely chopped
2 potatoes, peeled and finely
chopped
2 tomatoes, finely chopped
1 l / 2 ½ pints / 5 cups chicken stock
60 g / 1 ½ oz / ¼ cup macaroni pasta
40 g / 1 oz frozen peas
1 courgette, finely chopped
400g / 13 ½ oz / 1 ½ cups cod loin
salt and pepper
extra virgin olive oil

1. Heat the olive oil in a pan and cook the pancetta until the fat runs and it starts to turn golden.
2. Add the onion, carrot and celery and cook until softened and translucent.
3. Continue to add the potatoes and tomatoes and cook for a few minutes.
4. Add the stock and simmer for 30 minutes until all the vegetables are tender.
5. Once simmered, add the pasta and cook for a further 20 minutes.
6. Finish with adding the peas, courgette and gently lower the fish into the soup and cook for another 10 minutes.
7. Ladle into bowls to serve, drizzled with oil.

SERVES: **3-4** | PREP TIME: **45 MINS** | COOKING TIME: **10 MINS**

Pizza Four Seasons

FOR THE DOUGH
400 g / 13 ½ oz / 1 ½ cups strong white bread flour
100 g / 3 ½ oz / ½ cup fine ground semolina flour
½ tbsp salt
1 x 7 g sachet dried yeast
½ tbsp caster (superfine) sugar
350 ml / ½ pint / 1 ½ cups lukewarm water

FOR THE TOPPING, PER PIZZA
6 tbsp bottled passata
2 slices ham
3 button mushrooms, thinly sliced
6 black olives, stoned
4 artichoke hearts, halved
80 g / 3 oz / ¼ cup mozzarella
extra virgin olive oil

1. Pour the flours and salt into a bowl and make a well in the centre. Add the yeast and sugar, mix and leave for a few minutes. Once frothing, pour into the well.
2. Using a fork in a circular movement, slowly mix the flour into the water. When it starts coming together, use your hands to pat it into a ball.
3. Knead for 10 minutes, until it is smooth and elastic.
4. Flour and cover with film. Leave to rest for 30 minutes.
5. Roll the pizzas out 30 minutes before cooking.
6. Preheat the oven to 250°C (230° fan) / 500F / gas 9. Flour the surface, tear off a piece of dough and roll into a circle. Dust each circle with a little flour.
7. Spread the base of each with passata, then top each quarter with one of the ingredients and sprinkle the mozzarella cheese all over.
8. Place on a preheated baking sheet for 8-10 minutes until golden and crisp.

SERVES: 6-8 | PREP TIME: 30 MINS | COOKING TIME: 12 MINS

Mini Tomato Anchovy Tarts

1 pack ready-rolled puff pastry
1 tbsp butter
1 onion, peeled and finely chopped
2 cloves of garlic, finely chopped
200 ml / 6 ½ fl oz / ¾ cup passata
small handful oregano leaves
salt and pepper
1-2 ripe tomatoes, thickly sliced
8 black olives, stoned and halved
8 anchovy fillets

1. Preheat the oven to 200°C (180° fan) / 400F / gas 6.
2. Cut out pastry circles about 7cm in diameter from the sheet. You should make between 6 and 8.
3. Place on a greased baking sheet and bake in the oven for 12 minutes until crisp and golden.
4. When cooked, push the middle of each pastry circle down a little with a spoon to create a space for the filling.
5. Heat the butter in a pan and cook the onion and garlic until golden.
6. Add the passata and oregano and heat briskly until reduced and thick. Adjust the seasoning.
7. Spoon into the middle of the pastry cases, then top with a slice of fresh tomato.
8. Place the anchovy and 2 olive halves on top and grill until bubbling.
9. Leave to cool before eating.

SERVES: 6-8 | PREP TIME: 45 MINS | COOKING TIME: 8-10 MINS

Chicken and Cheese Pizzas

FOR THE PIZZA DOUGH

400 g / 13 ½ oz / 1 ½ cups strong white bread flour

100 g / 3 ½ oz / ½ cup fine ground semolina flour

½ tbsp salt

1 x 7 g sachet dried yeast

½ tbsp caster (superfine) sugar

350 ml / ½ pint / ⅓ cup lukewarm water

FOR THE TOPPING

1 onion, sliced

2 tbsp butter

2 chicken breasts, skinned and chopped

80 g / 3 oz / ⅓ cup Fourme d'Ambert cheese per pizza

1. Pour the flour and salt into a bowl and make a well.
2. Add the yeast and sugar to the water and mix. When frothing, pour into the well.
3. Bring in the flour from around the insides and mix into the water. When it starts to come together, pat it into a ball. Knead for 10 minutes, then flour the dough, cover with film and leave to rest for 30 minutes.
4. Cook the onion and butter in a pan until golden.
5. Add the chicken and cook until the chicken is golden and tender.
6. Roll the pizzas out 30 minutes before you want to cook them.
7. Preheat the oven to 250°C (230° fan) / 500F / gas 9. Flour the surface, tear off a piece of dough and roll into a circle about 0.5cm thick.
8. Dust each one with flour and lay out on the surface.
9. Top with the chicken, onions and sliced cheese. Place on a preheated baking sheet for 8-10 minutes until golden.

SERVES: **6** | PREP TIME: **15 MINS** | COOKING TIME: **10 MINS**

Veal Piccata with Courgettes

4 courgettes
6 veal escalopes
60 g / 2 oz / ½ stick butter
1 lemon, juiced
250 g / 9 oz / 1 ⅔ cups mascarpone
salt and pepper

1. Cut the courgettes into strips and steam for 5 minutes.
2. Place the veal escalopes between 2 sheets of cling film and pound with a rolling pin until thin.
3. Heat the butter in a pan until foaming, then sear the escalopes on each side for 2 minutes.
4. Season, add the lemon juice and increase the heat to reduce the liquid to a syrup. Pour over the escalopes.
5. Cut each escalope into 6 equal triangles.
6. Thread the escalopes onto a skewer, alternating with the courgettes, three to each skewer. Cover with foil to keep warm.
7. Add the mascarpone to the pan and deglaze. Season and pour in any resting juices from the veal.
8. Pour this mixture over the veal skewers and serve hot.

SERVES: 6-8 | PREP TIME: 10 MINS | COOKING TIME: 3 HOURS 45 MINS

Crostini with Bayonne Ham

4-5 ripe vine-grown plum tomatoes
1 ciabatta loaf, ready-to-bake
extra virgin olive oil
2 cloves of garlic, halved
300 g / 10 oz / 1 ¼ cups mozzarella
8 slices Bayonne ham
salt and pepper
basil

1. Preheat the oven to 100°C (80° fan) / 200F / gas 1. Slice the tomatoes in half and scoop out the seeds. Salt the insides and leave to drain.
2. Place in a roasting tin, drizzle with a little oil and bake for 3 hours. Remove from the oven and set aside.
3. Heat the oven and bake the ciabatta loaf according to packet instructions. Leave to cool and firm up.
4. When cool, cut the loaf into 1.5cm thick slices. Meanwhile slice the tomatoes and sprinkle with a little salt.
5. Heat a griddle pan and lay the bread on the griddle until you achieve char marks across both sides. If you don't have a griddle you can do this under the grill until the bread is lightly toasted.
6. Rub the toasted side with the cut garlic and drizzle with olive oil.
7. Lay half a slice of ham on each piece, then top with a little mozzarella.
8. Place a tomato half on top. Garnish with basil.

Beef Carpaccio with Mustard

250 g / 9 oz piece of beef fillet

FOR THE DRESSING
2 egg yolks
100 ml / 3 ½ fl. oz / ⅖ cup olive oil
½ lemon, juiced
1 tbsp mustard
handful rocket leaves
Parmesan shavings
1 tbsp capers, drained
extra virgin olive oil
salt and pepper

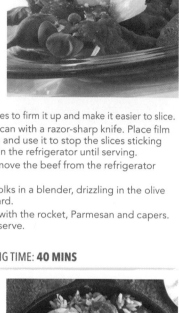

1. Place the fillet in the freezer for 30 minutes to firm it up and make it easier to slice.
2. Slice the fillet as thinly as you possibly can with a razor-sharp knife. Place film over each slice to prevent discolouring and use it to stop the slices sticking together. You can keep them this way in the refrigerator until serving.
3. Around 30 minutes before serving, remove the beef from the refrigerator and bring up to room temperature.
4. To make the dressing, whizz the egg yolks in a blender, drizzling in the olive oil. Season with lemon juice and mustard.
5. Lay the beef on a plate then decorate with the rocket, Parmesan and capers. Drizzle over the dressing. Season and serve.

Prawn and Chorizo Paella

1 litre / 1 pint 15 fl. oz / 4 cups chicken stock
1 pinch saffron
5 tbsp olive oil
1 onion, finely chopped
2 red peppers, diced
2 cloves of garlic, crushed
150 g / 5 ½ oz / 1 cup chorizo, halved and sliced
200 g / 7 oz / 1 cup paella rice
200 g / 7 oz / 1 cup raw prawns, peeled
1 small bunch flat leaf parsley, chopped

1. Heat the stock and saffron in a saucepan.
2. Heat the olive oil in a paella pan and gently fry the onion and peppers for 15 minutes. Add the garlic and chorizo and cook for 3 minutes.
3. Stir in the rice then let it toast for a minute. Pour in the hot stock and simmer without stirring for 10 minutes.
4. Distribute the prawns evenly into the liquid. Simmer for 5 more minutes.
5. Cover the pan with foil, turn off the heat and leave to stand for 5 minutes. Stir through the parsley and divide between four bowls.

SERVES: **4** | PREP TIME: **45-50 MINS** | COOKING TIME: **50-60 MINS**

Grilled Polenta with Antipasti

225 g / 9 oz / 1 cup polenta
1.7 l / 3 pints / 6 cups water
2 red peppers
olive oil
salt and pepper
2 handfuls, black olives, stoned
4 slices Parma ham
jar of artichoke hearts
Parmesan

1. Whisk the polenta slowly in a pan of boiling water. As soon as it begins to boil cover with a lid slightly askew and turn the heat down.
2. When it begins to thicken, stir every 5 minutes. Cook for 45 minutes until it develops the consistency of mashed potato and season generously.
3. Oil a tray and tip the polenta out onto to it. Spread the polenta 2.5cm thick. Leave it to cool for 30 minutes and then cut into squares.
4. Preheat the oven to 200°C (180° fan) / 400F / gas 7.
5. Cut the 'cheeks' off the peppers and roast in the oven with a little oil and seasoning until tender. Place in a plastic bag and leave for 20 minutes.
6. Peel the skins off the peppers when cool.
7. Cut the topping ingredients into bite-size pieces and use to top the polenta squares before serving.

SERVES: 6 | **PREP TIME: 20 MINS** | **COOKING TIME: 10 MINS**

Beef Tartare

500 g / 1 lb 2 oz pizza dough

2 onions, peeled and very finely chopped

1 shallot, peeled and very finely chopped

bunch of basil, chopped

1 tbsp Parmesan, grated

900 g / 2 lb / 6 cups beef fillet, finely chopped

5 tbsp olive oil

2 tbsp balsamic vinegar

salt and black pepper

1. Preheat the oven to 220°C (200° fan) / 425F / gas 7.
2. Roll out the pizza dough on a floured surface to about 1mm thick and cut into 12 small squares and place on greaseproof paper.
3. Bake in the oven for about 10 minutes or until crisp. When done, leave on a wire rack to cool.
4. Place the meat, onion, shallot, basil, olive oil and balsamic vinegar in a bowl and combine thoroughly, then season.
5. Spoon into 6 oiled circle moulds, pushing down gently.
6. Place 2 pizza squares on each plate, then top with the tartare. Decorate with Parmesan and a little more olive oil.

Lamb Meatballs

500 g / 1 lb 2 oz / 3 ⅓ cups minced lamb
1 onion, finely chopped
2 cloves of garlic, finely chopped
6 tbsp breadcrumbs
1 tbsp rosemary leaves, finely chopped
1 tbsp tomato purée
2 tbsp Parmesan, grated
½ lemon, zest grated
salt and pepper
2 tbsp olive oil

1. Place the minced lamb in a large bowl until it reaches room temperature.
2. Add the rest of the ingredients and mix well with your hands to ensure even distribution.
3. Roll the mixture into small balls with your hands and place on a baking tray. Cover with cling film and refrigerate for 30 minutes.
4. Heat the olive oil in a large pan.
5. Add the meatballs in batches, cooking on all sides until golden and just cooked through – about 6-8 minutes.
6. Serve with cooked rice and a tomato sauce.

Leek, Trout and Cheese Bake

12 lasagne sheets
200g / 6 ½ oz / ¾ cup smoked trout fillets
300 ml / 10 fl oz / 1 ¼ cups crème fraîche
½ bunch dill, finely chopped
zest and juice of ½ lemon
40g / 1 oz butter
4 leeks, trimmed and finely sliced

1. Cook the pasta in boiling salted water according to packet instructions.
2. Drain, brush over a little oil and keep warm.
3. Cook the leeks very gently in the butter with a sprinkling of salt until very soft and sweet.
4. Meanwhile flake the trout fillets into a bowl, removing any bones.
5. Gently mix with the creme fraiche, dill, lemon zest and a little juice. Season well.
6. Layer the lasagne sheets onto plates, 3 per serving. Spoon over the trout and crème fraîche filling, then top with leeks, then another layer of pasta and repeat.
7. Serve drizzled with extra virgin olive oil.

SERVES: **4** | PREP TIME: **20 MINS** | COOKING TIME: **1 HOUR 50 MINS**

Veal in Tomato Sauce

1.2kg / 2 lbs rose veal shin, cut into thick slices

3 tbsp olive oil

2 onions, peeled and finely chopped

200 g / 6 ½ oz / ¾ cup carrots, finely chopped

1 orange, grated zest

1 lemon, grated zest

1 clove garlic, finely chopped

400 g / 14 oz / 2 cups tomatoes

4 sage leaves

1 bouquet garni

2 tbsp basil, chopped

2 tbsp plain (all purpose) flour

200 ml / 6 ½ fl. oz / ¾ cup white wine

1 chicken stock cube

1. Heat the olive oil in a casserole pan and cook the onions and carrots until soft.
2. Add the garlic and cook for a minute, then the tomatoes, chopped sage leaves, bouquet garni and chopped basil and the citrus zest. Reduce the heat and cook over a very gentle heat for 15 minutes.
3. Dredge the veal slices in flour and sear in a hot pan for 2 minutes on each side in a little oil.
4. Add to the casserole pan.
5. Deglaze the frying pan with the white wine, scraping the base with a wooden spoon then pour into the casserole pan.
6. Crumble in the stock cube, top up with water to cover, cover with a lid and cook gently for 1 hour 30 minutes.
7. Remove the veal from the casserole, then push the sauce through a sieve for a smoother dish before serving.

Seafood Minestrone

1 tbsp olive oil
1 onion, peeled and finely chopped
1 carrot, peeled and finely chopped
1 celery stalk, peeled and chopped
2 tomatoes, finely chopped
1 L / 2 pints / 4 ¼ cups chicken stock
50 g / 1 ½ oz / ⅕ cup macaroni pasta
750 g / 1 ¼ lb / 3 cups mixed raw
    seafood, such as prawns, scallops,
    mussels and squid
1 bunch parsley, chopped
½ lemon
salt and pepper

1. Heat the olive oil in a pan and sweat the onion, carrot and celery without colouring for 5 minutes.
2. Add the tomatoes and cook for a further 2 minutes.
3. Pour over the stock, bring to a simmer and add the pasta.
4. Cook for about 20 minutes until the pasta is tender.
5. Add the seafood and poach in the soup until the prawns turn pink, the scallops opaque and the mussels open. Discard any that remain closed.
6. Scatter over the parsley and adjust the seasoning.

Ham, Tomato and Mozzarella Salad

4 ripe vine-grown tomatoes
2 buffalo mozzarella balls
salt and pepper
extra virgin olive oil
8 slices Parma ham
basil

1. Slice the tomatoes thickly, drizzle with oil and a little salt and leave to stand for 10 minutes.
2. Tear the mozzarella into pieces.
3. Arrange the tomatoes and mozzarella in an alternating pattern on a serving platter, drizzling over the juices from the tomatoes.
4. Lay the ham alongside.
5. Scatter over torn basil leaves and drizzle with more oil and a little pepper.

SERVES: **4** | PREP TIME: **10 MINS** | COOKING TIME: **40 MINS**

Scallop Fricassée with Polenta

FOR THE POLENTA

200 g / 7 oz / 1 cup polenta
1.5 l / 2 pints 12 fl. oz / 6 cups water
110 g / 4 oz / 1 stick butter
110 g / 4 oz / 1 cup Parmesan, grated

FOR THE SCALLOPS

40 g / 1 ½ oz / ⅓ stick butter
8 scallops, cleaned
salt and pepper
75 g / 3 oz / 1 cup girolle mushrooms, brushed clean
1 clove of garlic, finely chopped
½ lemon, juiced
¼ bunch parsley, chopped

1. Whisk the polenta into a pan of boiling salted water.
2. As soon as it begins to boil, cover loosely and turn the heat down to minimum.
3. When it begins to thicken, stir well every 5 minutes.
4. Cook for about 30 minutes then add a little water to get the consistency of thickly whipped cream.
5. Take off the heat, stir in the butter and Parmesan and season. Set aside and keep warm.
6. Heat the butter in a pan. Season the scallops. When the butter's foaming, place in the pan.
7. Add the mushrooms and garlic and cook for around 4-5 minutes, turning the scallops half way through.
8. Remove the scallops from the pan when opaque. Season the mushrooms and add the lemon and parsley.
9. Spoon the warm polenta onto a plate. Top with the mushrooms, then arrange the scallops on top.

MAKES: **2-3** | PREP TIME: **45 MINS** | COOKING TIME: **8-10 MINS**

Seafood Pizzas

FOR THE PIZZA DOUGH
400 g / 13 ½ oz / 1 ½ cups strong white bread flour

100 g / 3 ½ oz / ½ cup fine ground semolina flour

½ tbsp salt

1 x 7 g sachet dried yeast

½ tbsp caster (superfine) sugar

approx. 350 ml / ½ pint / ⅓ cup lukewarm water

FOR THE TOPPING
10 tbsp bottled passata

200 g / 6 ½ oz / ¾ cup raw prawns, shelled

1 scallop per pizza

handful black olives, stoned

1 green chilli, finely sliced

basil, to garnish

1. Pour the flours and salt into a bowl and make a well in the centre. Add the yeast and sugar to the water and mix. When frothing, pour into the well.
2. Slowly bring in the flour from around the insides and mix into the water. When it starts coming together, pat it into a ball. Knead for 10 minutes until smooth.
3. Flour the dough, cover with film and leave to rest for 30 minutes.
4. Preheat the oven to 250°C (230 ° fan) / 500F / gas 9. Flour the surface, tear off a piece of dough and roll into a circle about 0.5cm thick.
5. Dust each one with flour and lay out on the surface.
6. Spread 1 tbsp of passata on each pizza, and then top each one with the olives, prawns and chilli.
7. Slice the scallops in half and place into the prawns. Place on a preheated baking sheet for 10 minutes until golden.

Vegetable Dishes

SERVES: **4** | PREP TIME: **10 MINS** | COOKING TIME: **45 MINS**

Artichoke Antipasti

4 globe artichokes
lemon juice

FOR THE VINAIGRETTE
1 tsp salt
1 clove of garlic, crushed
1 tsp Dijon mustard
1 tbsp balsamic vinegar
black pepper
6 tbsp extra virgin olive oil

1. Remove around 4-5 of the toughest outer leaves. Snap away the stem.
   Spread the leaves apart until you come to the central thinner, lighter leaves.
   Pull this cone out in one piece and underneath will be the hairy choke;
   scrape out with a teaspoon.
2. Rinse the artichokes with water and place in a bowl of water with lemon juice
   to prevent discolouring.
3. To cook the artichokes, bring salted water to the boil with some lemon juice
   and cook, uncovered for about 30 minutes or until a leaf pulls away easily and
   the bases are tender when tested with a skewer.
4. Whisk together the first 5 ingredients to a smooth paste and then gradually
   stir in the olive oil until you have a smooth emulsion.
5. To eat the artichokes, serve at room temperature, tearing off a leaf at a time,
   dipping it into vinaigrette and eating the tender base, discarding the rest of
   the leaf. Eat the heart in the middle too.

Caprese Stuffed Tomatoes

6 large beef tomatoes

FOR THE FILLING
3 yellow tomatoes
3 green tomatoes
2 balls of buffalo mozzarella
100 g / 4 oz / ⅔ cup black olives, stoned
3 sprigs of basil
2 tbsp olive oil
salt and pepper

1. Slice the tops off the beef tomatoes and hollow out with a teaspoon.
2. Sprinkle the insides with a little salt and leave to drain upside down for 30 minutes, then pat dry.
3. Cut the yellow and green tomatoes into small chunks.
4. Dice the mozzarella.
5. Mix them together with the olives, olive oil, seasoning and basil.
6. Spoon mixture into the beef tomatoes and serve at room temperature.

Avocado with Tomato and Feta

2-3 ripe vine grown tomatoes
extra virgin olive oil
100 g / 3 ½ oz / ⅔ cup feta cheese
2 tbsp black olives, stoned
basil leaves
salt and pepper
2 ripe avocados
juice of ½ lemon, optional

1. Finely chop the tomatoes and place in a bowl. Season and drizzle with olive oil then leave to marinate for 10 minutes.
2. Dice the feta into small chunks, then add to the tomatoes, along with the olives. Tear up the basil leaves and add these too. Season to taste.
3. Cut the avocados in half when ready to serve and remove the stones.
4. Squeeze over a little lemon to prevent discolouring.
5. Fill the cavity in each avocado with the tomato and feta salad and serve.

SERVES: **4** | PREP TIME: **10 MINS** | COOKING TIME: **25 MINS**

Courgette Mousse

2 courgettes (zucchini), very
finely diced

1 egg, separated

1 heaped tbsp crème fraiche or
double (heavy) cream

100 g / 3 ½ oz Gruyère or Parmesan,
grated

salt and pepper

1 tbsp pesto

butter, for greasing the ramekins

2 tbsp pine nuts, lightly toasted

1. Preheat the oven to 200°C (180° fan)
   / 400F / gas 7.
2. Blanch the courgettes in boiling
   salted water for 3 minutes until
   tender.
3. Drain in a colander and then press
   lightly with a wooden spoon to
   extract excess water.
4. Whizz the courgettes in a blender
   with the egg yolk and crème fraiche
   until smooth. Season.
5. Whisk the egg white to a stiff peak
   and then fold gradually into the
   courgette mixture. Stir through
   the pesto.
6. Spoon into greased ramekins
   then bake in the oven for about
   20 minutes until set. Serve warm
   sprinkled with pine nuts.

Courgette, Feta and Tomato Bread

8 eggs
1 tbsp crème fraiche
2 courgettes (zucchini), finely diced
handful sun-dried tomatoes,
    finely chopped
100g / 4 oz / ⅔ cup feta cheese, cubed
6 sprigs thyme
2 tbsp olive oil

1. Preheat the oven to 180°C (160° fan) / 350F / gas 4.
2. Beat the eggs with the crème fraiche in a large bowl.
3. Add the courgettes, tomatoes, feta, thyme leaves and season then mix together carefully.
4. Oil a large frying pan, then pour the mixture in and bake for about 35 minutes until puffed and golden. The egg should be cooked through.
5. Cut into squares and serve warm or cold.

Creamed Yellow Pepper Soup

1 ciabatta loaf
olive oil
25 g / 1 oz butter
1 onion, finely chopped
1 clove of garlic, finely chopped
4 yellow peppers, finely chopped
750 ml / 1 ¼ pints / 3 cups chicken stock
120 ml / 4 fl oz / ½ cup double
    (heavy) cream
salt and pepper

1. Preheat the oven to 180°C / 350F / gas 5. Tear the ciabatta into large croutons and toss with olive oil. Place on a baking sheet.
2. Bake in the oven for 10-12 minutes, until golden and crunchy and then set aside on kitchen paper.
3. Heat the butter in a pan, then sweat the onion and garlic without colouring.
4. Add the peppers and cook for a further 10 minutes until they have softened.
5. Pour over the stock and simmer for 25 minutes, until the peppers are completely tender.
6. Allow to cool slightly and then whizz in a liquidizer until smooth.
7. Transfer back to the pan and stir in the cream, heating gently.
8. Adjust the seasoning before serving.

MAKES: **18** | PREP TIME: **10 MINS** | COOKING TIME: **40 MINS**

Italian-style Vegetables

1 aubergine (eggplant)
2 courgettes (zucchini)
2 red peppers, deseeded
2 onions, peeled
2 cloves garlic, whole
2 tbsp rosemary leaves, finely chopped
4 tbsp olive oil

1. Preheat the oven to 200°C (180° fan) / 400F / gas 6.
2. Slice the aubergine and courgettes into thick, even rounds about
   1cm (½ in.) in width.
3. Cut the peppers into large pieces.
4. Slice the onion into thick rings.
5. Tip the vegetables into a roasting tin and toss with the garlic, rosemary
   and seasoning and drizzle with oil.
6. Roast for about 30-40 minutes until all is tender and golden.

Farfalle Primavera

70 g / 2 ½ oz / ⅕ cup farfalle pasta
per person
olive oil
½ bunch asparagus, trimmed
100 g / 3 ½ oz / ½ cup peas, fresh
or frozen
100 g / 3 ½ oz / ½ cup broad beans,
double-podded
50g / 1 ½ oz / 1/5 cup butter
2 tsp Parmesan, grated
lemon juice
salt and pepper

1. Cook the pasta in boiling salted water according to packet instructions.
   Drain, reserving a little of the cooking water, then toss with little olive oil
   to prevent sticking.
2. Meanwhile steam the asparagus until nearly tender – check after 4 minutes,
   then keep checking.
3. Briefly cook the peas and beans for 2-3 minutes until just tender.
4. Heat the butter in a pan and add the vegetables. Cook for 1 minute then
   add the pasta and reserved water.
5. Toss together and then sprinkle over the Parmesan.
6. Adjust the seasoning and serve.

Grilled Red Peppers

4 red peppers
extra virgin olive oil
salt and pepper

1. Preheat a grill to very hot or open up a gas flame to full.
2. Roast the peppers under the grill or over the flame until completely
   blackened and blistered all over.
3. Place the peppers in a plastic bag and seal and set aside.
4. Once cool, peel the skin away from the flesh but try to keep the flesh intact.
5. Season and drizzle with olive oil. Serve with ciabatta to mop up the juices.

SERVES: **6** | PREP TIME: **30 MINS** | COOKING TIME: **25 MINS**

Salad with Soft-boiled Egg Dressing

2 red peppers
2 yellow peppers
Parmesan, to shave
120g / 4 ½ oz / ⅔ cup sun-dried tomatoes
175g / 6 oz / ¾ cup rocket (arugula) leaves
6 eggs
2 tbsp olive oil
2 tbsp balsamic vinegar
3 thick slices granary bread, cut in half

1. Cut the peppers in half and discard the seeds and white pith.
2. Lay on a baking sheet and grill until completely blackened. Remove from the heat, place in a plastic bag and leave to cool.
3. Peel the skin away from the peppers and roughly chop the flesh.
4. Place in a bowl with the rocket, tomatoes and some shaved Parmesan and set aside.
5. Cook the eggs in boiling water for 6 minutes. Remove, leave to cool a little then peel away the shell.
6. Dress the salad with the olive oil and balsamic vinegar. Season well.
7. Serve the salad with the egg just broken in half on top and the bread alongside.

SERVES: 6 | **PREP TIME: 40 MINS** | **COOKING TIME: 40-45 MINS**

Vegetable Tart

FOR THE TART
2 x 375 g packs ready-rolled
  shortcrust pastry
1 egg, beaten

FOR THE FILLING
olive oil
1 onion, peeled and finely chopped
2 cloves of garlic, finely sliced

1 aubergine (eggplant), cut into
  thin slices
2 courgettes (zucchini), cut into
  thin slices
1 jar roasted red peppers
2 eggs, beaten
275 ml / 10 fl oz / 1 cup double
  (heavy) cream
salt and pepper

1. Preheat the oven to 180°C (160° fan) / 350F / gas 4.
2. Roll out 1 pastry sheet and use to line a pie dish.
3. Heat the oil in a pan and cook the onion and garlic until golden.
   Move from the pan to a bowl using a slotted spoon.
4. Add the aubergine and a drop of oil and cook until tender,
   taking care to try to keep the slices intact. Place them on kitchen paper
   and repeat with the courgette slices.
5. Layer the vegetables with the peppers in the base of the pie dish,
   alternating the layers.
6. Whisk together the eggs and cream, season and pour over the vegetables.
7. Roll out the remaining pastry sheet and cut into 1cm wide strips. Use them
   to form a lattice on top of the pie.
8. Bake in the oven for around 35-40 minutes until the pastry is golden.
9. Serve warm.

Stuffed Mushrooms

4 large flat mushrooms
salt and pepper
olive oil
100g / 3 ½ oz / ½ cup Gorgonzola
2 tbsp mascarpone
handful flat leaf parsley

1. Season and drizzle the mushrooms with a little oil, then grill until tender.
2. Mix together the cheeses and parsley.
3. Spoon on top of the mushrooms and grill until the cheese is bubbling.
4. Serve with a rocket salad.

Sun-dried Tomato Cake

3 eggs
1 tsp sugar
225g /8 oz / 1 ½ cup plain (all purpose)
   flour
55 g / 2 oz / ⅓ cup potato flour
2 tsp baking (soda) powder
½ tsp salt
6 tbsp olive oil
2 tbsp sour cream
275 g / 10 oz / 1 ¾ cups sun-dried
   tomatoes, chopped
1 tsp paprika
1 tbsp thyme leaves, finely chopped

1. Preheat oven to 190°C / 375F / gas 5.
2. Whisk the eggs and sugar together until pale and thick.
3. Sieve the flours, baking powder and salt into a bowl, then fold into the eggs.
4. Stir in the sour cream and oil until incorporated.
5. Stir in the tomatoes, paprika and thyme leaves.
6. Grease and line four mini-loaf tins, then divide the mixture equally between them.
7. Bake in the oven for about 40 minutes until a skewer inserted into the middle comes out clean.
8. Remove to a wire rack and allow to cool.

MAKES: **2** | PREP TIME: **2 HOURS 40 MINS** | COOKING TIME: **20 MINS**

Olive and Tomato Focaccia

760g / 1 lb 10 oz/ 5 cups '00' flour
(Italian super-white flour)
½ tsp salt
2 tsp fast-action dried yeast
150 ml / 5 fl oz / ⅔ cup olive oil
450 ml / 16 fl. oz / 1 ⅘ cups
lukewarm water
150g / 5 oz / ⅔ cup mixed green and
black olives, pitted
150g / 5 oz / 1 cup cherry tomatoes
handful rosemary leaves
basil, to garnish

1. Sift the flour and salt into a bowl
and make a well. Pour 50ml of the
oil into the flour, add the yeast and
rub together. Pour in 3/4 of the
water and mix until the dough
comes together.
2. Tip the dough onto a floured
surface and knead for 10 minutes.
Place in a lightly oiled bowl,
cover with film and leave to rise in
a warm place for 1 hour 30 minutes.
3. Take the dough out of the bowl,
knock back and divide into two
balls. Roll into 2 circles and place
in oiled pizza pans. Cover and
leave for 30 minutes.
4. Preheat the oven to 200°C (180° fan)
/ 400F / gas 6.
5. Uncover the dough and push your
fingertips in at regular intervals to
make deep dimples. Drizzle
generously with oil so that the
dimples fill up.
6. Top with tomatoes, olives and
sprigs of rosemary. Sprinkle with
salt. Spray with a little water and
bake for 20 minutes. Drizzle with
oil and transfer to a wire rack to
cool before serving.

Penne with Spring Vegetables

500 g / 1lb / 2 cups penne pasta
2 tbsp butter, or olive oil
100 g / 3 ½ oz / ½ cup broccoli
8 asparagus stalks, woody ends
    snapped off and cut into short lengths
2 tsp Parmesan, grated

1. Cook the pasta in boiling salted water according to packet instructions.
2. Meanwhile heat the butter or oil in a pan and add the vegetables with a splash of pasta cooking water.
3. Cook gently until the broccoli and asparagus is just tender.
4. Drain the pasta and toss with the vegetables and keep warm.
5. Serve with grated Parmesan.

Polenta and Courgette Millefoglie

225 g / 9 oz / 1 cup polenta
1.7 l / 3 pints / 6 cups water
2 tbsp olive oil
2 courgettes (zucchini), finely diced
4 tbsp pine nuts, lightly toasted
6 mint leaves, finely sliced
zest of ½ lemon
salt and pepper

1. Whisk the polenta slowly in a pan of boiling water. As soon as it begins to boil, cover with a lid slightly askew and turn the heat down to minimum.
2. When it begins to thicken, stir every 5 minutes. Cook for 45 minutes until it begins to have the consistency of mashed potato. Season generously.
3. Oil a tray and tip the polenta out onto it. Spread the polenta to about 2.5cm thick.
4. Leave the polenta to cool for about 30 minutes and then cut into rectangles about 6cm x 4cm.
5. Meanwhile, heat the oil in a pan and fry the courgettes until tender.
6. Stir through the pine nuts, mint, zest and seasoning.
7. Spoon onto a polenta rectangle, top with another rectangle, and repeat. Set aside.
8. Repeat until the entire filling is used up.

Antipasti

4 red peppers
1 aubergine (eggplant)
2-3 tbsp extra virgin olive oil
1 tbsp balsamic vinegar
salt and pepper
1 tbsp pine nuts, lightly toasted
Parmesan shavings

1. Preheat a grill to very hot or open up a gas flame to full.
2. Roast the peppers under the grill or over the flame until completely blackened and blistered all over.
3. Place the peppers in a plastic bag and seal and set aside.
4. Repeat the process with the aubergine. Alternatively, you could roast the aubergine whole in a very hot oven until blackened and collapsed – about 1 hour.
5. Slice the aubergine in half and scoop out the middle into a bowl. Discard the skin.
6. Dress the aubergine with olive oil and balsamic vinegar and season. Peel the skin off the peppers. It should come away easily, but try to keep the flesh whole.
7. Lay the roasted pepper flat on a serving platter along with any juices from the bag.
8. Spoon the aubergine around and scatter over pine nuts and Parmesan before serving at room temperature.

MAKES: **3-4** | PREP TIME: **1 HOUR 20 MINS** | COOKING TIME: **30 MINS**

Pumpkin and Tomato Pizzas

FOR THE PIZZA DOUGH
400 g / 14 oz / 2 ⅔ cups strong white bread flour

100 g / 3 ½ oz / ⅔ cup fine ground semolina flour

½ tbsp salt

½ tbsp dried yeast

½ tbsp caster (superfine) sugar

350ml / 12 fl. oz / 1 ⅖ cups lukewarm water

FOR THE TOPPING
1 butternut squash, halved and deseeded

1 tbsp olive oil

20 cherry tomatoes, halved

2 balls mozzarella

handful basil leaves

1. To make the pizza, pour the flours and salt into a bowl and make a well in the centre, add the yeast and sugar to the water, mix with a fork and leave for a few minutes.
2. Bring in all the flour, working your way towards the outer edges, mixing well.
3. When it starts to come together, use your hands and pat it into a ball.
4. Knead the dough for around 10 minutes until the dough is smooth and elastic, cover with film and leave to rest for 30 minutes.
5. Preheat the oven to 240°C (220° fan) / 475F / gas 9.
6. Cut the butternut squash into small chunks and roast for about 20 minutes in the oven with the olive oil until tender and caramelised.
7. Roll the pizzas out about 30 minutes before you want to cook them. Then flour the surface, tear off a piece of dough and roll into a rough circle of about 1cm (½ in) thick.
8. Top each pizza with some of the butternut squash, halved tomatoes and small pieces of mozzarella.
9. Place either directly on the bars of the oven or on a preheated baking sheet for 8-10 minutes until golden and crisp. Sprinkle with basil leaves before serving.

SERVES: **4** | PREP TIME: **10-15 MINS** | COOKING TIME: **40-45 MINS**

Polenta and Lentil Croquettes

FOR THE CROQUETTES
1.2 l / 2 pints / 5 ½ cups vegetable oil
200 g / 7 oz / 1 cup green lentils
200 g / 7 oz / 1 cup polenta
110 g / 4 oz / 1 cup smoked tempeh
    110 g / 4 oz / ⅔ cup plain flour
2 medium eggs, beaten
1 tbsp miso paste, dissolved in 750 ml
    / 1 pint 6 fl. oz / 3 cups hot water
1 tsp turmeric
salt and pepper

GARNISH
2 chicory bulbs, leaves removed
55 g / 2 oz / ½ cup bulgar wheat
1 tbsp sunflower seeds
1 tsp chilli (chili) flakes
small handful of micro salad
basil

1. Combine the lentils, turmeric, miso and hot water mixture and seasoning in a saucepan.
2. Bring to the boil over a moderate heat and cook for 10 minutes before reducing to a simmer for 15-20 minutes.
3. Remove from the heat and mash until smooth.
4. Spoon into a bowl and add the cornflower and tempeh, cover and chill.
5. Place the bulgar in a saucepan and cover with boiling water.
6. Cook over a very low heat, until the grains are plump and tender.
7. Drain if necessary and season to taste.
8. Heat the oil in a saucepan to 180°C (160° fan) / 350F gas 4.
9. Spoon the lentil mixture and shape into croquettes.
10. Dust in the flour then dip in the beaten egg.
11. Coat in the polenta before arranging on lined trays.
12. Deep-fry in the hot oil until golden.
13. Drain on kitchen paper and spoon the bulgar into the chicory leaves, arranging next to the croquettes.
14. Garnish the bulgar with sunflower seeds, salad and a pinch of chilli flakes before serving.

Pumpkin Gnocchi

400 g / 13 ½ oz / 1 ½ cups pumpkin,
   peeled
250 g / 9 oz / 1 cup potatoes, peeled
2 eggs
500 g / 1 lb / 2 cups flour
salt and pepper

1. Cut the pumpkin and potato into
   cubes and steam for 30-45
   minutes, until tender.
2. Push through a potato ricer to
   make a smooth puree, or mash
   thoroughly until there are no lumps.
3. Add the eggs, mix well, then add
   the flour and stir until completely
   combined. The mixture should be
   fairly stiff and you should be able
   to shape it.
4. Form into small balls and press
   down lightly on one side with a
   fork to give the gnocchi shape.
5. Bring a large pan of salted water
   to the boil and tip in the gnocchi.
   When they float to the surface,
   they are cooked, so remove with
   a slotted spoon and leave to
   drain on kitchen paper.
6. Reheat immediately in a pan,
   with butter and Parmesan or
   your favourite pasta sauce.

Penne with Tomato and Olives

400 g / 14 oz / 4 cups penne
100 ml / 3 ½ fl. oz / ½ cup olive oil
2 cloves of garlic, crushed
6 anchovy fillets in oil
400 g / 14 oz / 2 cups canned plum
    tomatoes
½ tsp dried oregano
150 g / 5 ½ oz / 1 cup mixed pitted
    olives, drained
75 g / 2 ½ oz Pecorino Romano,
    in one piece
4 sprigs basil

1. Boil the pasta according to the packet instructions.
2. Meanwhile, heat the oil in a sauté pan with the garlic and anchovies, stirring until the anchovies dissolve.
3. Add the tomatoes and let it come to a simmer. Stir in the oregano and olives.
4. Drain the pasta and stir it into the sauce. Divide between four bowls, then use a vegetable peeler to shave over the Pecorino. Garnish with basil and serve immediately.

Mushroom and Tomato Salad

400g / 13 ½ oz / 1 ½ cups button
    mushrooms, brushed clean
300g / 10 oz / 1 ¼ cups cherry
    tomatoes, preferably on the vine
3 tbsp olive oil
4 cloves of garlic, lightly crushed

FOR THE DRESSING
4 tbsp extra virgin olive oil
1 tbsp balsamic vinegar
1 sprig lemon thyme

1. Preheat the oven to 200°C (180° fan) / 400F / gas 7.
2. Place the mushrooms and tomatoes in a roasting tin and toss with the oil. Arrange the garlic cloves around the vegetables.
3. Roast in the oven for about 30 minutes.
4. Tip the contents of the pan into a serving bowl, reserving the cooking juices.
5. Pour the cooking juices into a bowl. Pick out the garlic cloves and squeeze into the bowl.
6. Whisk in a little more extra virgin olive oil and the balsamic.
7. Add the thyme then gently toss the warm vegetables in the dressing.

Stuffed Red Peppers

4 red bell peppers, cored and seeded

FOR THE FILLING
4 tsp olive oil
100 g / 4 oz / ½ cup risotto rice
1 red bell pepper, chopped
2 cups broccoli florets
1 small courgette (zucchini), chopped
1 cup mixed olives, sliced
500 ml / 18 fl. oz / 2 cup vegetable stock
2 sprigs of thyme, roughly chopped

1. Preheat the oven to 180°C (160° fan) / 350F / gas 4.
2. Cook peppers for 4 minutes in boiling water, or until just softened.
3. Heat the oil. Fry the rice over a low heat, stirring frequently for 2 minutes before adding the remaining vegetables. Continue for 2 more minutes.
4. Pour in the stock and cook for 15 minutes, stirring until the rice is tender.
5. Drain off any excess liquid, then stir in the thyme. Season to taste.
6. Spoon the stuffing into the peppers and then place in a roasting tin.
7. Bake in the oven for about 20 minutes or until the peppers are tender and the stuffing is hot.

Tomatoes with Ratatouille

8 tbsp olive oil
2 tomatoes, chopped
1 small aubergine (eggplant), finely chopped
2 courgettes (zucchini), finely chopped
1 red pepper, seeded and finely chopped
salt and pepper
8 tomatoes
100 g / 3 ½ oz / ½ cup black olives, stoned
2 sprigs of basil

1. Heat half the oil in a large pan then add the aubergine and pepper and cook for 10 minutes.
2. Then add the courgettes, stir well, reduce the heat and cook for a further 10 minutes.
3. Finally, add the tomatoes, season, cover and cook for 15 minutes.
4. Cut the olives into rounds and then add to the pan with the basil.
5. Preheat the oven to 210°C (190° fan) / 420F / gas 7.
6. Take the tops off the tomatoes and hollow out with a teaspoon.
7. Place in a roasting tin and fill each one with ratatouille. Place the tops back on, drizzle with the rest of the oil and cook in the oven for about 25 minutes.
8. Serve hot or warm.

Roasted Aubergine with Tomatoes

2 large aubergines (eggplants) or 4 small ones
salt
2 tbsp olive oil
4 tomatoes, chopped
1 tbsp balsamic vinegar

1. Preheat the oven to 200°C (180° fan) / 400F / gas 6.
2. Slice the aubergines in half lengthways. Cut the flesh into a cross hatch with a small sharp knife, then salt lightly and leave upside down for 20 minutes. This will help them absorb less oil.
3. Turn the aubergines right way up and pat dry. Drizzle generously with oil, then top with tomatoes and season with black pepper.
4. Roast in the oven for about 30 minutes, or until the flesh is completely tender and the tomatoes have sunk into the aubergines.
5. Drizzle with a little balsamic before serving.

SERVES: **6** | PREP TIME: **1 HOUR 15 MINS** | COOKING TIME: **3-4 MINS**

Mushroom Ravioli

FOR THE PASTA
500 g / 1 lb 2 oz / 3 ⅓ cups '00' flour
6 eggs

FOR THE FILLING
3 tbsp butter
200 g / 7 oz / 2 ⅔ cup wild
  mushrooms, brushed clean
150 g / 5 oz / 2 cups flat mushrooms,
  finely chopped
½ onion, peeled and finely chopped
2 tbsp Parmesan, grated
1 tbsp flat leaf parsley, finely chopped
salt and pepper

GARNISH
butter
Parmesan, grated

1. Place the flour in a bowl and make a well in the centre. Crack the eggs into the well.
2. Beat the eggs, then draw in the flour until the dough comes together. Knead the dough for 5 minutes. Cover with film and rest for 30 minutes in the refrigerator.
3. Heat the butter and sweat the onion and mushrooms. Stir in the Parmesan and parsley and season.
4. Using a pasta machine, roll the dough into sheets 2mm thick and 10cm wide. Lay on a floured surface.
5. Place 1 tsp of filling in the middle of the sheet at one end. Repeat all the way along at 5cm intervals and then brush a little water in a circle, around each filling.
6. Place another sheet of pasta on top, then push the sheets together and around each mound of filling.
7. Cut the ravioli into shapes.
8. Bring a large pan of salted water to the boil and cook for 3-4 minutes. Remove carefully with a slotted spoon then toss with more butter and Parmesan to serve.

Roasted Aubergines

2 aubergines (eggplants)
2 tbsp olive oil
2 tsp dried oregano

1. Preheat the oven to 200°C (180° fan) / 400F / gas 6.
2. Slice the aubergines in half lengthways and place in a roasting tin.
3. Using a sharp knife, score a cross hatch pattern into the flesh. This will help them cook more quickly.
4. Drizzle generously with good olive oil and season. Sprinkle over the oregano.
5. Roast in the oven for 25-30 minutes or until blackened and collapsed.
6. The flesh can now be scooped out and used as a dip or blended with yogurt or cream cheese for a milder flavour.

Red Pepper Involtini

4 red peppers
olive oil

FOR THE FILLING
100g / 3 ½ oz / ½ cup pine nuts
100g / 3 ½ oz / ½ cup cream cheese
1 tbsp Parmesan, grated
½ bunch flat leaf parsley
zest of 1 lemon
salt and pepper

1. Preheat the oven to 200°C (180° fan) / 400 F/ gas 7.
2. Seed and core the pepper and then roast whole with a little oil until tender but not too blackened.
3. Open out the peppers and cut each one into 2 rectangles and set aside.
4. Toast ¾ of the pine nuts in a dry frying pan until lightly golden.
5. Add to a food processor with the cream cheese, Parmesan, parsley, zest and a little seasoning and whizz until smooth.
6. Stir in the whole pine nuts.
7. Spoon the filling down one side of each pepper rectangle, then roll the pepper up to make a roulade.
8. Serve at room temperature.

Side Dishes

Arancini with Pine Kernels

275g / 10 oz / 1 cup cooked arborio rice, cold
1 tbsp Parmesan, grated
4 tbsp pine nuts
1 tbsp plain (all purpose) flour
1 egg, beaten
40g / 1 ½ oz / ⅓ cup breadcrumbs
vegetable oil, for deep frying

1. Stir the Parmesan through the risotto.
2. Toast the pine nuts in a dry pan until lightly golden. Stir through the risotto.
3. Shape into equal balls.
4. Lay out the flour, egg and breadcrumbs on separate plates.
5. Dip the risotto balls into the flour, then the egg, then the breadcrumbs. Use one hand and keep the other clean for ease.
6. Heat the oil to 180°C / 400F or until a cube of bread sizzles when dropped in the oil. Fry the risotto balls until golden and crisp all over.
7. Serve hot or warm.

Italian Bread

450ml / 1 pint / 2 cups water
210g / 7 oz / ¾ cup chickpea (gram) flour
3 tbsp olive oil
½ tsp salt
1 tsp rosemary leaves, finely chopped

1. Mix the water with the chickpea flour, 1 tbsp oil and the salt in a large bowl.
2. Cover and leave to rest for 2 hours.
3. Preheat the oven to 200°C (180° fan) / 400F / gas 6.
4. Heat a large oven-proof frying pan with the remaining oil.
5. Skim off any foam from the batter and stir in the rosemary.
6. Pour the batter into the pan and place in the oven for 25 minutes until brown and crisp.
7. Sprinkle with sea salt before serving.

SERVES: **4** | PREP TIME: **25 MINS** | COOKING TIME: **10-15 MINS**

Breaded Cheese Balls

10 slices white bread, crusts removed
125 g / 4 ½ oz / 1 cup mozzarella pearls
285 g / 10 oz / jar artichoke hearts
6 tbsp plain (all purpose) flour
3 eggs, beaten
10 tbsp vegetable oil, for frying

1. Combine the bread with salt and pepper in a food processor to make breadcrumbs.
2. Drain the mozzarella pearls and artichoke hearts. Pat dry.
3. Tip the flour onto one plate and the eggs into a shallow bowl.
4. Coat the mozzarella pearls and artichokes in the breadcrumbs.
5. Dunk the crumbed cheese and artichokes into the egg, then the flour, then the egg again.
6. Heat the oil in a pan until a cube of bread sizzles when dunked in.
7. Fry cheese and artichokes in the oil in batches, turning carefully, until golden and crisp on all sides.
8. Drain on kitchen paper and serve hot.

Tomato and Basil Crostini

1 ficelle
olive oil
40 cherry tomatoes
2 sprigs rosemary leaves, finely chopped
2 cloves of garlic, halved
bunch basil leaves
extra virgin olive oil

1. Preheat the oven to 200°C (180° fan) / 400F / gas 7. Place the cherry tomatoes in a roasting tin and drizzle with oil, salt and pepper. Sprinkle over the herbs and roast in the oven for about 25 minutes or until lightly charred and wizened.
2. Slice the ficelle into rounds about 1cm (½ in) thick.
3. Dab each one with a little oil and bake in the oven until lightly golden and crisp, for about 8 minutes.
4. Rub the crostini with the garlic. Push the tomatoes to one side in the tin and lightly press each crostini into the roasting juices to soak into the bread a little.
5. Top each crostini with a cherry tomato and sprinkle over the basil.

SERVES: 6 | PREP TIME: 1 HOUR 25 MINS | COOKING TIME: 5 MINS

Ricotta Fritters

3 large eggs

600g / 1 lb 5 oz / 4 cups ricotta cheese

½ tsp paprika

125g / 4 ½ oz / ¾ cup plain (all-purpose) flour

2 red peppers, seeded and finely diced

1 handful chives, finely chopped

vegetable oil, for frying

basil, to garnish

1. Separate 2 eggs and place the whites in the refrigerator for later use.
2. Place the ricotta in a bowl, season with salt and pepper and add the paprika – whisk in 1 whole egg and the 2 yolks a little at a time.
3. Whisk in the flour and then combine until smooth. Cover with film and place in the refrigerator for 1 hour.
4. Whisk the reserved egg whites to stiff peaks with a pinch of salt.
5. Add the red pepper and chives to the ricotta mixture, then gently mix in the egg whites, being careful not to lose the air.
6. Heat the oil in a pan. Using a teaspoon dipped in hot water, dip teaspoons of the mixture into the oil and turn gently until golden all over. Do this in batches.
7. Remove to kitchen paper to drain and keep warm in a low oven until required.

MAKES: **6-8** | PREP TIME: **15 MINS** | COOKING TIME: **8 MINS**

Bruschetta

1 ciabatta loaf
extra virgin olive oil
2 cloves of garlic, halved
300 g / 10 oz / 1 ¼ cups mozzarella
5 very ripe vine-grown tomatoes,
   room temperature
black olives, chopped
salt and pepper
basil

1. Preheat the oven and bake the ciabatta loaf according to packet instructions. Once cooked, leave to cool.
2. When cool, cut the loaf into 1.5cm thick slices.
3. Meanwhile slice the tomatoes and sprinkle with a little salt.
4. Heat a griddle pan until very hot and lay the bread on the griddle. If you don't have a griddle, you can do this under the grill until the bread is lightly toasted.
5. Rub the toasted side with the cut garlic and drizzle with olive oil.
6. Slice the mozzarella and lay with the tomatoes on the toasted bread and scatter with chopped olives.
7. Scatter over the basil before serving.

SERVES: **4** | PREP TIME: **25 MINS** | COOKING TIME: **3 HOURS 35 MINS**

Confit Tomatoes with Baked Ricotta

500 g/ 1 lb 2 oz / 3 ⅓ cups plum tomatoes
6 cloves garlic, unpeeled
4 thyme and 4 rosemary sprigs
6 tbsp olive oil
500g / 1 lb 2 oz / 3 ⅓ cups ricotta
2 eggs
1 tbsp Parmesan, grated
½ lemon, grated zest
1 tbsp oregano leaves, chopped

1. Preheat the oven to 120°C (100° fan) / 250F / gas ½.
2. Halve the tomatoes and place in a roasting tin. Scatter over the garlic and herbs and drizzle with oil.
3. Slow-roast in the oven for 3 hours until shrivelled and intense in flavour.
4. They can be preserved in a sterilised jar covered in oil in the refrigerator.
5. Tip the ricotta into a bowl and stir with a wooden spoon to loosen slightly.
6. Beat in the eggs one at a time, then add the Parmesan, zest and oregano. Season.
7. Tip into a greased loaf tin and bake at 180°C / 350F / gas 5 for 35 minutes or so until set.
8. Leave to cool then tip out onto a serving platter.
9. Serve the ricotta with the confit tomatoes and bread.

Garlic Bread

2 baguettes
120g / 4 oz / 1 stick butter, softened
4 cloves garlic, crushed
1 tbsp parsley, finely chopped
225 g / 8 oz / 2 cups Fontina cheese

1. Slice the baguettes on a diagonal to get elongated slices.
2. Mix the butter thoroughly with the garlic and parsley.
3. Spread the butter thickly onto the bread.
4. Top with slices of cheese and flash under a hot grill until bubbling and golden.

Mozzarella Panzerotti

FOR THE PIZZA DOUGH
200 g / 6 ½ oz / ¾ cup strong white
   bread flour
50 g / 1 ½ oz / ⅕ cup fine ground
   semolina flour
¼ tbsp salt
½ x 7g sachet dried yeast
¼ tbsp caster (superfine) sugar
175 ml / ¼ pint / ¾ cup lukewarm water

FOR THE FILLING
100g / 3 ½ oz / ½ cup mozzarella
   cheese, cut into small cubes
200 ml / 6 ½ fl oz / ¾ cup passata
3 tbsp basil, chopped
vegetable oil for deep frying

1. For the pizza dough, pour the flours and salt into a bowl, making a well in the centre. Mix the yeast, sugar and water and pour into the well. Bring the flour into the water. When it comes together, pat it into a ball. Knead for 10 minutes. Cover and leave to rest for 30 minutes.
2. Meanwhile, mix together the filling ingredients.
3. Once the dough has risen, uncover it and pull it out, using your hands, until it is thin. Cut out about 15 little circles with a cutter or an upturned cup.
4. Place 1 tsp of the filling onto half of the pastry circle. Fold the other half over, pinching to seal. Repeat.
5. Heat the oil to 190°C (170° fan) / 375F / gas 5. Deep fry the panzerotti in batches for around 5 minutes until puffed and golden.
6. Drain on kitchen paper and season. Serve hot.

SERVES: **4** | PREP TIME: **1 HOUR** | COOKING TIME: **10 MINS**

Gnocchi with Nutmeg and Cheese

700g floury potatoes, such as Maris Piper, peeled
250g plain (all purpose) flour
1 egg, beaten
nutmeg, grated to taste
4 tbsp butter
4 sage leaves
3 tbsp Parmesan, grated
100g / 3 ½ oz / ½ cup Gruyère cheese, grated

1. Boil the potatoes whole in boiling salted water for at least 25 minutes until completely tender all the way through.
2. Drain and mash thoroughly – or use a potato ricer – until completely smooth. Leave to cool.
3. Tip the cooled potatoes into a bowl and work in the flour, egg, a pinch of salt and nutmeg until you have a smooth dough.
4. Cut the dough in half and roll out to make 2 fat sausages.
5. Cut into pieces about 3cm long and press down gently with the tines of a fork to make the traditional indentations. Place on a floured baking sheet to cook when ready.
6. To cook the gnocchi, bring a large pan of salted water to the boil then add the gnocchi. When they float to the top, they are ready, so remove and drain on kitchen paper.
7. Heat the butter in a pan then toss the gnocchi and sage leaves in the butter.
8. Tip into a baking dish and scatter with Parmesan and Gruyère.
9. Grill until bubbling and golden.

Rustic Tomato Soup

2 tbsp olive oil
1 onion, peeled and chopped
1 carrot, peeled and finely chopped
1 celery stalk, finely chopped
2 cloves of garlic, chopped
1 courgette, finely chopped
2 potatoes, peeled and finely chopped

2 slices Parma ham, chopped
400 g / 14 oz / 2 cups canned chopped tomatoes
1 dried red chilli, chopped
1 l / 1 pint 16 fl. oz / 4 cups chicken stock
salt and pepper
extra virgin olive oil

1. Heat the oil in a pan and sweat the onion, carrot and celery without colouring.
2. Add the garlic and cook for 2 minutes until soft.
3. Add the courgettes and potatoes, stir well and then leave to soften for 5-10 minutes, then add the ham.
4. Pour in the tomatoes, crumble in a little of the chilli, then stir in the stock.
5. Bring to a simmer and leave to cook until the vegetables are tender – about 20 minutes.
6. Taste and adjust the seasoning if necessary, adding chilli if desired.
7. Roughly mash the vegetables with a potato masher or pulse in a liquidizer.
8. Serve drizzled with olive oil.

SERVES: **4** | PREP TIME: **20 MINS** | COOKING TIME: **10 MINS**

Mozzarella Arancini

60g / 2 oz / ¼ cup leftover risotto (Arborio) rice, cooked
1 tbsp Parmesan, grated
1 ball mozzarella, cut into small cubes
1 tbsp basil leaves
1 tbsp plain (all purpose) flour
1 egg, beaten
4 tbsp breadcrumbs
vegetable oil, for deep frying

1. Leave the leftover risotto to get completely cold – preferably refrigerated overnight.
2. Stir the tomato and Parmesan through the risotto.
3. Shape into equal balls, pushing a small cube of mozzarella into the centre of each one and shaping the rice around it.
4. Lay out the flour, egg and breadcrumbs on separate plates.
5. Dip the risotto balls into the flour, then the egg, then the breadcrumbs. Use one hand and keep the other clean for ease.
6. Heat the oil and fry the risotto balls until golden and crisp all over.
7. Serve hot or warm.

MAKES: 12 | PREP TIME: 10 MINS | COOKING TIME: 45 MINS

Italian Gougères

110g / 4 oz / ⅔ cup plain (all-purpose) flour

½ tsp salt

½ tsp black pepper

½ tsp dried oregano

pinch cayenne pepper

250 ml / 9 fl oz / 1 cup milk

125g / 4 ½ oz / 1 ⅛ sticks butter, cubed

6 eggs, 1 separated

2 tbsp Parmesan, grated

4 tbsp Gruyère, grated

2 tbsp milk

4 tomatoes, sliced

handful of black olives, stoned and sliced

½ bunch basil leaves, chopped

1. Preheat the oven to 220°C (200° fan) / 450F / gas 7.
2. Place the flour in a bowl with the salt, pepper, oregano and cayenne.
3. Add the milk and butter to a large pan and bring to the boil. When the butter melts, reduce the heat and tip in the seasoned flour.
4. Stir quickly and vigorously with a wooden spoon, beating until the dough starts to come away from the sides of the pan and form a ball.
5. Remove the pan from the heat and tip into a large mixer bowl. Beat at a medium speed for 1 minute, then the eggs one at a time, beating until each one is absorbed before adding the next.
6. Beat in the cheeses.
7. Fill a piping bag with the mixture and use to pipe onto ungreased baking trays.
8. Lightly press a tomato slice, a few chopped olives and basil into the centre of each one.

Whisk the remaining egg yolk with the milk and lightly brush the gougères.

9. Bake for about 10 minutes, then reduce the heat to 150°C / 300F / gas 2 and bake for a further 15 minutes, or until golden brown.
10. Cool on wire racks before serving.

Pesto Mozzarella Arancini

275g / 10 oz / 1 cup cooked arborio
  rice, cold
1 tbsp Parmesan, grated
4 tbsp pesto
1 ball mozzarella, cut into small cubes
1 tbsp plain (all purpose) flour
1 egg, beaten
4 tbsp breadcrumbs
vegetable oil, for deep frying

1. Stir the Parmesan, pesto and mozzarella through the risotto.
2. Shape into equal balls. If you prefer, you could make finger shapes instead.
3. Lay out the flour, egg and breadcrumbs on separate plates.
4. Dip the risotto balls into the flour, then the egg, then the breadcrumbs.
   Use one hand and keep the other clean for ease.
5. Heat the oil to 180°C / 400F or until a cube of bread sizzles when dropped
   in the oil. Fry the risotto balls until golden and crisp all over.
6. Serve hot or warm.

Mozzarella Fritters

6 slices white bread, crusts removed
salt and pepper
pinch dried chilli flakes
1 ball mozzarella
3 heaped tbsp plain (all purpose) flour
2 eggs, beaten
vegetable oil, for frying

1. Mix the bread with salt and pepper and the chilli flakes in a food processor to
   make breadcrumbs.
2. Slice the mozzarella into 0.5cm slices
3. Tip the flour onto one plate and the eggs into another.
4. Coat the mozzarella slices in the breadcrumbs.
5. Dunk the crumbed slices into the egg, then the flour, then the egg again.
6. Heat about 1cm (½ in) depth of oil in a pan until a cube of bread sizzles when
   dunked in.
7. Fry the crumbed mozzarella in the oil, turning carefully, until golden and crisp
   on all sides.
8. Drain on kitchen paper and serve hot.

MAKES: **40** | PREP TIME: **30-40 MINS** | COOKING TIME: **8 MINS**

Mushroom Crostini

1 ficelle
olive oil
250g / 9 oz / 1 cup mushrooms
1 onion, peeled
2 tbsp butter
2 cloves of garlic, very finely chopped
nutmeg
salt and pepper
juice of ½ lemon
2 tbsp double cream, to bind

1. Preheat the oven to 180°C (160° fan) / 350F / gas 5.
2. Slice the ficelle into rounds about 1cm thick.
3. Dab each one with a little oil and bake in the oven until lightly golden and crisp, for about 8 minutes.
4. Whizz the mushrooms and onion in a food processor until finely chopped.
5. Heat the butter in a pan and cook the mushrooms and onions with the garlic for about 25-30 minutes until all the water has evaporated.
6. Season and stir in enough cream just to bind.
7. Top the crostini with the mushroom mixture.

SERVES: 4 | PREP TIME: 25 MINS | COOKING TIME: 15 MINS

Spinach and Mozzarella Cake

250g / 9 oz / 1 cup spinach leaves, washed

150g / 5 oz / ⅔ cup mozzarella

4-6 floury potatoes, cooked and mashed (leftovers are perfect)

1 egg yolk

150g / 5 oz / ⅔ cup plain flour

pinch paprika

olive oil

1. Wilt the spinach leaves in a pan, then leave to cool. Drain as thoroughly as possible, then finely chop and set aside.
2. Drain the mozzarella then cut into small cubes.
3. Place the mashed potato in a bowl, then mix in the egg yolk, followed by the spinach and mozzarella. Season with salt and pepper.
4. Pat the mixture into small rounds or cakes.
5. Mix the flour with a little seasoning and paprika, then dredge the cakes in it.
6. Heat about 1cm (½ in) depth of oil in a pan, then cook the cakes on both sides until golden and crisp.
7. Drain on kitchen paper and serve hot.

SERVES: **4** | PREP TIME: **20 MINS** | COOKING TIME: **45 MINS**

Caponata Stuffed Aubergine

2 aubergines (eggplants)

4 tbsp olive oil

1 tsp dried oregano

1 onion, peeled and finely chopped

2 cloves of garlic, peeled and finely sliced

2 celery stalks, chopped

bunch of flat leaf parsley, chopped

2 tbsp capers, drained

12 green olives, stoned

3 tbsp red wine vinegar

4 ripe tomatoes, chopped

salt and pepper

1. Preheat the oven to 200°C (180° fan) / 400F / gas 6.
2. Cut the aubergines in half lengthways, drizzle with 2 tbsp oil and bake in the oven for about 30 minutes until tender.
3. Remove the flesh with a spoon, leaving the skin intact and with a margin of flesh to support the structure.
4. Heat the rest of the olive oil in the pan and cook the onion with oregano, garlic and celery until softened.
5. Add the aubergine and the rest of the ingredients and simmer for around 15 minutes until the vinegar has evaporated.
6. Season and spoon into the aubergine skins.
7. Serve immediately.

SERVES: **4** | PREP TIME: **2 HOURS** | COOKING TIME: **25 MINS**

Rocket and Parmesan Focaccia

FOR THE DOUGH
360 g / 12 ½ oz / 2 ⅓ cups '00' flour
¼ tsp salt
1 tsp fast-action dried yeast
75 ml / 3 fl. oz / ⅓ cup extra-virgin
  olive oil
250 ml / 9 fl. oz / 1 cup lukewarm
  water

FOR THE FILLING
100 g / 4 oz / 1 ⅓ cups rocket (arugula)
  leaves
75 g / 3 oz / ⅔ cup pine kernels
4 tbsp Parmesan cheese, grated
black pepper

1. Sieve the flour into a bowl with the salt and make a well.
2. Add the yeast and 50ml / 2 fl. oz olive oil and rub together.
3. Pour in the water and mix until the dough comes together.
4. Tip the dough onto a floured surface and knead for about 10 minutes,
    pushing it away from you with the heel of your hand until the dough
    feels smooth and elastic.
5. Place in a lightly oiled bowl covered with film and leave for 1 ½ hours.
6. Preheat the oven to 220°C (200° fan) / 425F / gas 7.
7. Uncover the dough and knead until smooth. Roll two-thirds into a circle
    about 30cm wide and line a cake tin, lining the extra over the top.
8. Arrange the rocket leaves, Parmesan and pine kernels over the base.
    Grind black pepper and drizzle with oil.
9. Roll the remaining dough into a circle measuring about 25cm. Lift onto
    the pie and press the edges together, sealing with water.
10. Trim the excess dough and brush with olive oil, bake for 35 minutes.

SERVES: 6 | **PREP TIME: 1 HOUR 20 MINS** | **COOKING TIME: 50 MINS**

Ricotta and Spinach Cake

500g / 1 lb 2 oz / 4 ½ cups spinach, washed
1 clove garlic, crushed
40g / 1 ½ oz / ⅓ stick butter
300g / 10 ½ oz / 2 cups plain (all-purpose) flour
5 eggs
200g / 7 oz / 1 ⅓ cups Ricotta
150g / 5 oz / 1 ½ cups Parmesan, grated
nutmeg, grated to taste

1. Wilt the spinach with the garlic in the butter. Season and cook until all the water has evaporated from the pan. Chop and set aside.
2. Place the flour, 3 eggs and a pinch of salt in a mixing bowl of a food processor and mix until they just come together to form a ball.
3. Remove from the bowl and work with your hands for 1 minute to make a smooth elastic dough. Wrap in film and leave in the refrigerator for 1 hour.
4. Roll out the pastry onto a floured surface, turning a quarter turn regularly to ensure you make a rectangle around 2mm thick.
5. Mix the ricotta with the Parmesan, a pinch of salt and pepper and a little grated nutmeg, then whisk in 2 beaten eggs and then work in the spinach.
6. Spoon the mixture down one side of the pastry, then roll up to make a cylinder shape.
7. Wrap the entire cake in foil very tightly and securely and steam for about 45 minutes or until cooked. Allow to rest for 10 minutes.

SERVES: 4 | PREP TIME: 30 MINS | COOKING TIME: 12 MINS

Italian Appetisers

1 sheet ready rolled puff pastry
4 tbsp tapenade
8 sun-blushed tomato pieces
1 cucumber
4 tbsp mascarpone
3 tbsp pesto
1 tbsp pine nuts, lightly toasted
1 baguette or ciabatta
4 tbsp fruit chutney
4 slices Parma ham

1. Preheat the oven to 200°C (180° fan) / 400F / gas 6. Cut out 8 circles from the puff pastry, 5cm in diameter.

2. Place on a greased baking sheet and bake in the oven for about 10-12 minutes or until puffed and golden.

3. Remove from the oven and push down the centre of each circle to make a well in which to put the filling.

4. Once cool, spoon in a little tapenade and top with a sun-blushed tomato.

5. Run a vegetable peeler down the length of the cucumber to create an alternating striped effect.

6. Cut the cucumber into rounds about 2cm thick.

7. Mix together the mascarpone, pesto and pine nuts, then spoon a little onto each round of cucumber.

8. Slice the baguette into eight 2 ½cm (1 in) thick rounds and lightly toast under a grill.

9. Spoon a little fruit chutney on each one and top with a torn piece of Parma ham, folded into a rose shape.

SERVES: **4** | PREP TIME: **35 MINS** | COOKING TIME: **55 MINS**

Polenta and Olive Chips

200g / 7 oz / 1 cup polenta
1.5 l / 2 pints 12 fl. oz / 6 cups water
130g / 4 ½ oz / 1 ¼ cups Parmesan, grated
2 handfuls black olives, stoned and chopped
oil for deep frying

1. Whisk the polenta slowly into a large pan of boiling salted water.
2. As soon as it begins to boil, stir every 5 minutes, ensuring you push the spoon down into the sides of the pan.
3. Cook for about 45 minutes until it begins to have the consistency of mashed potato. Season generously and stir in the Parmesan and olives.
4. Oil a tray and tip the polenta out onto it. Spread the polenta to about 2.5cm thick
5. Leave the polenta to cool for about 30 minutes, then cut into chip shapes when firm.
6. Heat the oil to 180°C / 400F or until a cube of bread sizzles when dropped in the oil, deep fry the polenta chips in batches until golden and crisp.
7. Drain on kitchen paper and sprinkle with salt before serving.

Mini Pizza Appetisers

FOR THE PIZZA DOUGH
400 g / 14 oz / 2 ⅔ cups strong white
  bread flour
100 g / 3 ½ oz / ⅔ cup fine ground
  semolina flour
½ tbsp salt
1 x 7 g sachet dried yeast
½ tbsp caster (superfine) sugar
350 ml / 12 fl. oz / 1 ⅖ cup lukewarm
  water

FOR THE TOPPING
bottled passata
anchovies
black olives, stoned
small handful rocket leaves
2 tbsp pine kernels
basil, to garnish

1. Pour the flour and salt into a bowl and make a well in the centre.
2. Add the yeast and sugar to the water, mix with a fork and leave for a
   few minutes. Pour into the well.
3. Bring in the flour from around the insides and mix into the water.
   When it starts coming together, use your hands and pat it into a ball.
4. Knead the dough for 10 minutes. Flour the dough, cover with film and leave
   to rest for 30 minutes.
5. Preheat the oven to 240°C (220° fan) / 475F / gas 9. Flour the surface, tear
   off a piece of dough and roll into a rough rectangle or square.
6. Dust each one with a little flour and lay out on the surface.
7. Spread passata on each one, then top with olives, anchovies and rocket.
8. Sprinkle with pine kernels and place on a baking sheet. Bake for 8-10 minutes
   until golden.

Polenta Galettes

200 g / 7 oz / 1 cup polenta
1.5 l / 2 pints 12 fl. oz / 6 cups water
130 g / 4 ½ oz / 1 ¼ cups Parmesan, grated

1. Whisk the polenta slowly into a large pan of boiling salted water.
2. As soon as it begins to boil, cover loosely with a lid and turn the heat down as low as possible.
3. When it begins to thicken, stir well every 5 minutes or so, ensuring you push the spoon down into the sides of the pan.
4. Cook for about 45 minutes until it begins to have the consistency of mashed potato. Season generously and stir in the Parmesan.
5. Oil a tray and tip the polenta out onto it. Spread the polenta to about 2.5cm thick.
6. Leave the polenta to cool for about 30 minutes and then cut circles out 5cm in diameter. Top with anything you fancy.

MAKES: 2 | PREP TIME: 2 HOURS 40 MINS | COOKING TIME: 20 MINS

Olive Focaccia

750g / 1 lb 10 oz / 5 cups '00' flour
(Italian super-white flour)
½ tsp salt
2 tsp fast-action dried yeast
150 ml / 5 fl oz / ⅔ cup olive oil
450 ml / 16 fl. oz / 1 ⅘ cups lukewarm
water
200g / 7 oz / 1 ⅓ cups mixed olives,
pitted and chopped
handful rosemary leaves

1. Sift the flour and salt into a bowl
   and make a well in the centre.
   Pour 2 tbsp of the oil into the flour,
   add the yeast and rub together
   with your fingers.
2. Pour in about 3/4 of the water and
   mix until the dough comes together.
   Tip the dough onto a floured
   surface and knead for 10 minutes
   until smooth and elastic.
3. Place in a lightly oiled bowl, cover
   with film and leave to rise in a warm
   place for 1 hour 30 minutes.
4. Take the dough out and punch out
   the air. Work the olives into the
   dough. Divide into two balls.
5. Roll into 2 circles and place in
   2 lightly oiled pizza pans.
6. Cover with film and leave to rise for
   30 minutes.
7. Preheat the oven to 200°C (180°
   fan) / 400F / gas 6. Uncover the
   dough and push your fingertips in
   to make deep dimples. Drizzle with
   oil so that the dimples fill up.
   Top with sprigs of rosemary.
   Sprinkle with salt.
8. Spray with water and bake for
   20 minutes. Drizzle with oil and
   transfer to a wire rack to cool
   before serving.

Desserts

SERVES: **6** | PREP TIME: **30 MINS** | CHILLING TIME: **3 HOURS**

Strawberry and Pistachio Tiramisu

500 g / 1 lb 2 oz / 2 cups of mascarpone

125 g / 4 ½ oz / ½ cup of caster (superfine) sugar (⅘ for mascarpone and ⅕ for strawberries)

350 g / 12 oz / 1 ½ cups of strawberries

30 g / 1 oz of pistachio paste

6 egg yolks

250 ml / 8 fl. oz / 1 cup of whipping cream

20 finger biscuits

120 ml / 4 fl. oz / ½ cup of milk

crushed pistachios and mint leaves for decoration

1. Separate the eggs then mix the yolks and 100 g / 3 ½ oz of sugar until frothy.
2. Add the mascarpone and separate in 2 bowls.
3. Whip the cream until stiff and add to the 2 mixtures.
4. Blend half the strawberries with 25 g / 1 oz of sugar, then combine with one of the mascarpone mixtures. Combine the other mix with the pistachio paste.
5. Soak the finger biscuits in the milk and line the bottom of the serving dishes with half of them.
6. Top with the mascarpone mixture with pistachio, then half the remaining strawberries and the remaining biscuit.
7. Top with the strawberry mascarpone mixture and the rest of the strawberries, crushed pistachios and mint leaves. You can caramelize the pistachio for added crunch.
8. Chill for 3 hours.

SERVES: **8** | PREP TIME: **20 MINS** | RESTING TIME: **5 HOURS**

Panna Cotta with Toffee

1 l / 2 pints / 4 cups whipping cream
110 g / 4 oz / ½ cup caster
  (superfine) sugar
2 gelatine sheets
1 vanilla pod

FOR THE TOFFEE SAUCE
110 g / 4 oz / ½ cup light brown sugar
120 g / 4 oz / ½ cup butter
90 ml / 3 fl. oz / ⅓ cup milk

FOR THE ALMOND TOFFEE
450 g / 1 lb / 2 cups caster
  (superfine) sugar
pinch salt
200 g / 7 oz / 2 cups flaked
  (silvered) almonds
120 ml / 4 fl. oz / ½ cup water

1. Soak the gelatine sheets in cold water. Drain them and reserve. Boil the cream with the sugar and vanilla pod cut in its length.
2. Turn off the heat and add the gelatine, stirring. Strain the cream then let it cool, stirring often. Pour the cream into serving glasses and keep in fridge for 5 to 6 hours.
3. In the meantime, prepare the toffee sauce by melting the butter and sugar in a saucepan over low heat until the sugar dissolves (without burning).
4. Stir in the cream gently until boiling then stir and let cool before pouring on top of the set panna cotta.
5. To prepare the almond brittle stir together the sugar, water and salt in a saucepan and cook over medium heat until golden brown then remove from the heat and stir in the almonds.
6. Pour the mixture on a baking tray the let cool for about 15 minutes before breaking into pieces.

Cherry Mascarpone Ice Cream

250 ml / 8 fl. oz / 1 cup double cream
400 g / 13 oz mascarpone
250 ml / 8 fl. oz / 1 cup cane sugar syrup
25 preserved cherries
cherry syrup
basil, to garnish

1. Whip the cream until very stiff (but not churned).
2. Whisk the mascarpone with the sugar cane syrup.
3. Fold in the whipped cream and then the preserved cherries.
4. Pour into a silicone cake mould and cover with plastic wrap.
5. Press down well and freeze for at least 6 hours.
6. Unmould, slice and serve with cherry syrup.

Raspberry Tiramisu

250 g / 9 oz of raspberries
500 g / 1 lb 2 oz of mascarpone
110 g / 4 oz / ½ cup of caster (superfine) sugar
2 eggs, separated
12 finger biscuits
150 ml / 5 fl. oz / ½ cup of Marsala
cocoa powder, to serve

1. Mix the mascarpone with the sugar and beaten eggs yolks.
2. Whisk the egg whites to soft peaks and fold into the egg yolk mixture.
3. Puree the raspberries and keep a few for decoration.
4. Place the raspberry coulis at the bottom of the serving dishes.
5. Dip the finger biscuits in Marsala and place them over the raspberry coulis.
6. Add the mascarpone mixture, then dust with cocoa powder.
7. Finish with the fresh raspberries and chill for 2 hours.

SERVES: **6** | PREP TIME: **30 MINS** | COOKING TIME: **30 MINS**

Zuppa Inglese

250 g / 9 oz plain panettone or brioche
4 eggs
100 g / 4 oz sugar
500 ml / 1 pt / 2 cups whole milk
75 g / 3 oz cornstarch
125 g / 4 ½ oz dark chocolate
1 tsp of instant coffee

1. Heat ¾ of the milk, ¼ of the sugar and the chocolate until completely melted, then incorporate the cornstarch and cook until the mixture thickens.
2. Let the mixture cool, stirring occasionally, then incorporate the coffee and stir.
3. Pre-heat the oven to 180°C (160°C fan) / 350F / gas 4.
4. Meanwhile, cut the brioche and soak it in a mix of the remaining milk, 1 egg and 3 egg yolks.
5. Place half the soaked brioche in the bottom of a buttered dish, then top with the chocolate / coffee cream then with the rest of the brioche.
6. Cook for 15 minutes, until the brioche firms up. Meanwhile, beat the remaining 3 egg whites until very stiff, then add the remaining sugar and beat again until the sugar is dissolved.
7. Let the cake cool down, then cover with the egg white mixture and place in the oven for 5 minutes under the grill. The meringue should just start to brown.

Chocolate Ice Cream

250 g / 9 fl. oz / 1 cup evaporated milk
250 ml / 9 fl. oz / 1 cup of milk
3 egg yolks
150 g / 5 oz full fat plain yogurt
4 tbsb sugar
150 g / 5 oz of dark chocolate

1. Mix the evaporated milk with the milk in a saucepan and heat without boiling.
2. Mix the sugar and egg yolk and pour the egg mixture gently into the hot milk mixture, stirring constantly. Cook for 10 minutes.
3. Melt the chocolate over a bain-marie then slowly incorporate the chocolate to the milk.
4. Remove from the heat and let cool to room temperature.
5. Add the yogurt and mix well, then refrigerate.
6. Churn for 40 minutes in an ice cream maker or place in the freezer for 4 hours, whisking regularly until frozen.

Panna Cotta with Raspberries

1 l / 2 pts / 4 cups whipping cream
110 g / 4 oz / ½ cup sugar
3 gelatine sheets
1 vanilla pod
For the coulis and serving
500 g / 1 lb 2 oz / 2 cups raspberries
200 g / 7 oz / 1 cup sugar
8 mint leaves, for decoration

1. Soak the gelatine in cold water, drain and reserve.
2. Boil the cream with the sugar and vanilla pod cut in its length.
3. Turn off the heat and add the gelatine, stirring.
4. Strain the cream and let it cool, stirring often.
5. Pour the cream into the serving dishes or glasses and keep in the fridge for 5 hours.
6. Prepare the coulis by mixing the cleaned raspberries (minus a handful for decoration) and the sugar. Keep in the fridge.
7. Before serving, unmould the panna cotta or serve it in its pretty glass with the raspberry coulis and fresh raspberries and mint leaves.

SERVES: **6** | PREP TIME: **4 HOURS 20 MINS** | COOKING TIME: **10 MINS**

Tiramisu and Raspberry Sorbet

400 g / 14 oz of mascarpone

500 ml / 1 pt of raspberry sorbet

400 g / 2 cups of raspberries

4 tbsp of crème fraiche

120 g / 5 oz of icing (confectioner's) sugar

12 finger biscuits

150 ml / 5 fl. oz / 2 / 3 cup of Marsala water

6 mint leaves for decoration

1. Boil 2 / 3 of the Marsala and 200ml / 7 fl. oz of water. Cool and filter.
2. Whisk the mascarpone in a bowl with the crème fraiche, half the icing sugar and remaining Marsala.
3. Mash half the raspberries with the remaining sugar then filter to get rid of the pips and get a smooth raspberry coulis.
4. Dip the finger biscuits into the Marsala mixture.
5. Place half the mascarpone mixture in the serving dishes, then the finger biscuits and half the raspberry coulis.
6. Top with the rest of the mascarpone cream and the rest of the coulis. Sprinkle with the remaining raspberries.
7. Put the tiramisu in the fridge for at least 4 hours.
8. Serve well chilled with a scoop of raspberry sorbet and some mint leaves.

SERVES: **6** | PREP TIME: **15 MINS** | COOKING TIME: **1 HOUR**

Gingerbread and Orange Tiramisu

300 g / 10 ½ oz / 2 cups plain flour

160 g / 5 ½ oz / 1 ½ sticks butter

75 g / 3 oz / ⅓ cup golden
 caster sugar

110 g / 4 oz / ⅓ cup golden syrup

125 g / 4 ½ oz / ½ cup honey

1 large egg

175 ml / 6 fl. oz / ¾ cup milk

1 ½ tsp ground ginger

500 ml / 1 pint / 2 cups whipping
 cream

250 g / 9 oz / 1 cup mascarpone

75 ml / 3 fl. oz / ⅓ cup Marsala

75 g / 3 oz / ⅓ cup caster sugar

1 orange, diced into small chunks

225 g / 8 oz / 1 cup caster sugar

250 ml / 9 fl. oz / 1 cup cold water

1. Preheat the oven to 180°C (160°C fan) / 350F / gas 4.
2. Grease a tin and line with greaseproof paper. Sift together the flour and
   ground ginger.
3. Whisk the butter and sugar until fluffy. Beat in the honey and golden
   syrup and mix 2 tbsp of the flour mixture and beat the egg in.
4. Fold in the flour, then follow with the milk. Spoon into the tin and bake for
   45 minutes. Combine the water and sugar in a pan and cook over a low heat.
5. Simmer for 5 minutes before adding the orange and cook for 10 minutes.
   Arrange on a baking tray. Remove the gingerbread and let it cool, then
   slice into triangles.
6. Combine the cream, mascarpone, Marsala and sugar in a bowl and whisk.
   Spread the cream into the base of a glass dish. Arrange the triangles on top.
   Sprinkle the top with the cocoa powder.

Lemon Polenta Flan

250 ml / 8 fl. oz / 1 cup of cream
500 ml / 1 pt / 2 cups of milk
150 g / 5 oz of sugar
4 eggs
125 g / 4 ½ oz of polenta
1 lemon
a vanilla pod

1. Pre-heat the oven at 180°C (160° fan) / 350F / gas 4.
2. Mix the cream, milk, sugar, water, lemon juice and zest, polenta, vanilla pod and eggs together.
3. Whisk to obtain a homogeneous cream.
4. Heat on medium heat, stirring constantly with a whisk.
5. After about 10 minutes, the preparation will thicken.
6. Turn off the heat and pour the mixture into a buttered flan tin.
7. Cook for 25 minutes in the oven and cool in the refrigerator for 2 hours.
8. Serve cold or slightly warmed.

Polenta and Sage Madeleines

100 g / 4 oz ½ cup plain
  (all purpose) flour
80 g / 3 oz / ⅓ cup caster
  (superfine) sugar
2 tbsp polenta
2 eggs
1 tsp baking powder
150 ml / 5 fl. oz / ⅔ cup olive oil
1 lemon, juiced
handful sage leaves, finely sliced

1. Preheat the oven to 200°C (180° fan) / 400F / gas 6.
2. Oil a Madeleine mould tray and line a sage leave at the bottom of each Madeleine shape
3. In a bowl, beat the eggs until frothy. Still beating, add the sugar, flour and baking powder.
4. Stir in olive oil and the thinly sliced sage and carry on beating.
5. Finish by adding the polenta and lemon juice.
6. Once the mixture is smooth, fill the moulds with the batter and bake for 15 to 20 minutes. Check they are cooked with a knife point.
7. Serve the Madeleines with jam or grated coconut and chocolate sauce.

SERVES: **6** | PREP TIME: **20 MINS** | COOKING TIME: **40 MINS**

Pipasena Italian Cake

450 g / 1 lb flour
200 g / 7 oz sugar
25 cl / 8 fl. oz / 1 cup of milk
125 g / 4 ½ oz butter
2 eggs
125 g / 4 ½ oz raisins
125 g / 4 ½ oz candied fruits
1 lemon
2 tbsp dark rum
1 tsp baking powder
1 sachet of vanilla sugar
3 tbsp oil

1. Pre-heat the oven to 190°C (170° fan) / 375F / gas 5.
2. Mix the raisins, candied fruits, rum and a little water in a bowl to marinate them.
3. Heat in the microwave oven for 1 minute and let cool.
4. Grate the zest of lemon.
5. Heat the milk and butter until the butter is melted.
6. Mix the flour and baking powder, add the eggs, then the warmed milk mixture.
7. Add the sugar, vanilla sugar and oil.
8. Fold in the grated zest and drained fruits and raisins gently.
9. Cook for 40 minutes.

MAKES: **18** | PREP AND REST TIME: **45 MINS** | COOKING TIME: **15 MINS** |

Cappuccino Cream Dessert

1 litre / 2 pts milk
125 g / 4 ½ oz sugar
50 g / 2 oz cornstarch
50 g / 2 oz cappuccino powder mix
25 g / 1 oz unsweetened bitter cocoa
30 cl / 10 fl. oz liquid whipping cream
1 tbsb icing (confectioner's) sugar
chocolate sauce
mozzarella
basil, to garnish

1. Mix all the powders (cornstarch, sugar, unsweetened cocoa mixture and cappuccino) with cold milk.
2. Bring to a boil in a heavy saucepan and let thicken, stirring to prevent the bottom of the cream burning.
3. Once the desired consistency of the cream is reached (usually just before boiling), remove from the heat and add half the cream.
4. Leave to cool at room temperature for about 30 minutes, stirring occasionally.
5. Meanwhile, whisk the rest of the cream until stiff then add the icing sugar and whisk a bit more.
6. Place the cream in pretty cups, and top with chantilly cream with a piping bag and a sprinkle of chocolate sauce.

Ricotta Cake

250 g / 9 oz of ricotta
150 g / 5 oz of caster (superfine) sugar
150 g / 5 oz of plain (all purpose) flour
3 eggs
60 ml / 2 fl. oz / ¼ cup of milk
1 lemon, grated zest and juiced
pinch powdered ginger

1. Pre-heat the oven to 200°C (180° fan) / 400F / gas th.6.
2. Put in the bowl the ricotta, eggs, sugar and ginger, then whip until smooth.
3. Add the grated lemon zest and juice, beat again.
4. Add the flour gradually.
5. Pour the batter into a buttered and floured pan.
6. Cook in the oven for 30 to 40 minutes. When cooked, the cake should be puffed and golden.
7. Serve warm or cold.

Panforte di Sienna

100 g / 4 oz candied fruit peel (oranges or lemons)
100 g / 4 oz liquid honey
100 g / 4 oz caster (superfine) sugar
50 g / 2 oz plain (all purpose) flour
75 g / 3 oz blanched hazelnuts (cob nuts)
75 g / 3 oz blanched almonds
50 g / 2 oz cocoa powder
¼ tsp of ground cinnamon
¼ tsp of allspice powder
icing (confectioner's) sugar for decoration

1. Preheat the oven to 160°C / 315F / gas 3.
2. Finely chop the zest, and mix with the hazelnuts and almonds.
3. Mix everything in a bowl with the flour, cocoa, all spice and cinnamon.
4. Prepare a syrup: pour the honey and sugar in a saucepan. Heat over low heat until the sugar dissolves and bring to a boil, stirring constantly, until the mix forms a ball.
5. Remove from the heat and pour into the bowl, and combine everything.
6. Line a cake pan with a sheet of baking paper and smooth the dough to 2cm (1 in) thick. Place in the oven and bake for 30 to 35 minutes.
7. When the cake is golden brown, let it cool.
8. Just before serving, dust with icing sugar passed through a fine sieve.

Strawberry Zabaglione

500 g / 1 lb / 2 cups strawberries
150 g / 5 oz / 2 / 3 cup caster (superfine) sugar
100 g / 4 oz / ½ cup honey
125 g / 4 ½ oz / ½ cup mascarpone
1 lemon
3 eggs
1 tsp cardamom seeds
100 ml / 3 ½ oz / ½ cup double (heavy) cream
2 tbsp white balsamic vinegar
250 ml / 8 fl. oz / 1 cup water
6 mint leaves

1. Wash and hull the strawberries and cut them in two. Mix them with the juice of half the lemon and a tablespoon of caster sugar and reserve.
2. Boil half the remaining sugar, water, vinegar and half the cardamom seeds to make a syrup.
3. In another saucepan, caramelize the honey with the remaining cardamom and zest of lemon.
4. Mix the flavoured honey with the syrup, then refrigerate. After cooling, filter and sprinkle half the strawberries and marinate for twenty minutes. Reserve.
5. Break the eggs, add the remaining sugar and beat until white and compact. Beat the cream until stiff, mix with the cheese and add to the previous mixture.
6. Arrange the fruit in syrup at the bottom of the serving dishes and top with the mascarpone cream.
7. Finish with the remaining strawberries and fresh mint leaves for serving.

SERVES: **4** | PREP TIME: **4 HOURS 15 MINS** | COOKING TIME: **15 MINS**

Rhubarb Tiramisu

FOR THE MASCARPONE CREAM
200 g / 7 oz of mascarpone
100 g / 4 oz of caster (superfine) sugar
1 egg, separated

FOR THE RHUBARB COMPOTE
5 large stalks of rhubarb
110 g / 4 oz of brown sugar

FOR THE BASE
110 g / 4 oz / 1 stick of butter
200 g of cinnamon finger biscuits

1. To prepare the mascarpone cream, mix the egg yolk, sugar and mascarpone and stir in the egg white, after beating it until stiff. Then chill.

2. Wash and chop the rhubarb stalks. Cook them with the sugar in a covered pan over low heat, stirring occasionally with a wooden spoon. Reserve.

3. Prepare the base by blending 150g / 5oz of cinnamon biscuits and combining it with the softened butter.

4. Place the biscuit base in serving dishes, then half the mascarpone cream and the rhubarb compote.

5. Crumble a couple of biscuits on top of the rhubarb, then the rest of the mascarpone cream.

6. Chill in the fridge for at least 4 hours.

7. Just before serving, the dishes can be sprinkled with cocoa powder, crumbled biscuits or a pinch of cinnamon powder.

SERVES: **10** | PREP TIME: **15 MINS** | COOKING TIME: **15 MINS**

Polenta and Chocolate Chip Cookies

1 egg
3 tsp brown sugar
3 tsp butter
2 tbsp instant polenta
2 tbsp plain (all purpose) flour
½ tsp baking powder
2 tbsp chocolate chips

1. Preheat the oven to 180°C / 350F / gas 4.
2. In a bowl, whisk the egg with the sugar then add the butter and mix well.
3. Add the polenta (without cooking it before), flour and baking powder.
4. Once the mixture is smooth, take a tablespoon of dough, quickly forming a ball with your fingers and place on a baking sheet. Flatten with a spoon to form the cookie.
5. Space the cookies well on the sheet.
6. Cook for 15 minutes, then add the chocolate chips (they should stick to the cookies but not melt).
7. Remove from the oven and transfer to a wire rack to cool.

Semifreddo

450 ml / 16 fl. oz / 2 cups cream
3 eggs and 4 egg yolks
2 tbsp vanilla extract
4 tbsp sugar
4 tbsp Cointreau liqueur
1 tbsp orange zest

1. In a pan over low heat, mix the eggs, egg yolks, sugar and vanilla for 5 minutes until the mixture is thickened.
2. Remove from the heat and let cool.
3. In a bowl, whisk the cream until stiff then incorporate to the cooled egg mixture.
4. Add the Cointreau and orange zest.
5. Place the mixture in glasses and freeze for at least 4 hours.
6. Remove from the freezer about 15 minutes before serving (the mixture needs to start melting slightly).
7. Serve with chocolate pearls, orange zest or caramel shards.

Bilberry Tiramisu

4 Madeleine cakes
250 g / 9 oz of mascarpone
120 ml / 4 fl. oz / ½ cup of double (heavy) cream
200 g / 7 oz of bilberries
3 egg yolks
110 g / 4 oz of caster (superfine) sugar
60 g / 2 ½ oz of poppy seeds
60 g / 2 ½ oz of brown sugar
A pinch of cinnamon
1 tbsp of Amaretto
4 tbsp of Marsala

1. Mix the bilberries with sugar and cinnamon. Cool and refrigerate for 1 hour, stirring occasionally.
2. In a bowl, whisk the mascarpone with the egg yolks, sugar, poppy seeds and amaretto.
3. Add the cream after whipping it until stiff. Cool and refrigerate.
4. Line the bottom of each glass with broken Madeleine soaked in Marsala.
5. Place a first layer of mascarpone cream, then the bilberries with cinnamon.
6. Cover with a second layer of cream.
7. Sprinkle with poppy seeds and cinnamon powder.
8. Cool and refrigerate for 2 hours before serving.

SERVES: **8** | PREP TIME: **30 MINS** | CHILLING TIME: **4 HOURS**

Chocolate Tiramisu

500 g / 1 lb 2 oz of mascarpone
200 g / 7 oz of dark chocolate
150 g / 5 oz of caster (superfine) sugar
250 ml / 8 fl. oz / 1 cup of milk
4 eggs
30 finger biscuits
cocoa powder, for dusting
8 chocolate squares
2 tbsp rum (optional)

1. Mix the mascarpone with the sugar and egg yolks until it forms a homogeneous cream.
2. Reserve half of the mixture.
3. Melt the chocolate over a bain-marie with half the milk and a tablespoon of rum, let cool slightly and add half the mascarpone mix.
4. Beat the egg whites until stiff and stir in half in the mascarpone cream and half in the chocolate mixture.
5. Add a tbsp of rum to the remaining milk.
6. Dip the biscuits in this mixture and place half of them at the bottom of the individual serving dishes.
7. Cover with half the mascarpone cream, a couple of tbsps of the chocolate mix, then the rest of the mascarpone cream.
8. Carry on with the rest of the finger biscuits, the remaining chocolate mix and finish off with cocoa powder and a square of dark chocolate.
9. Chill for up to 4 hours in refrigerator.

SERVES: **4** | PREP TIME: **10 MINS** | COOKING TIME: **90 MINS** | RESTING TIME: **1 HOUR**

Sienna Nougat with Fruit

350 g / 12 oz blanched almonds
250 g / 9 oz liquid honey
225 g / 8 oz / 1 cup of sugar
200 g / 7 oz hazelnuts
3 egg whites
1 lemon and its zest
25 cl / 8 fl. oz / 1 cup of cream
1 tbs icing (confectioner's) sugar
100 g / 4 oz / ½ cup redcurrants
100 g / 4 oz / ½ cup raspberries
mint leaves

1. Place the honey in a bowl over a bain-marie and simmer for 10 minutes stirring regularly.
2. Meanwhile, pre-heat the oven to 200°C (180°C fan) / 400F / gas 6.
3. Grill the almonds and hazelnuts for 1 minute, checking regularly to ensure they don't burn. Reserve.
4. In a pan, make a caramel with the sugar and 100ml / 3 fl. oz of water.
5. Beat the egg whites until stiff then incorporate gently in the honey mixture.
6. Add the caramel and mix thoroughly for 5 minutes.
7. Add the hazelnuts, almonds, lemon zest and juice.
8. Pour the mixture on a rectangular tray lined with baking paper.
9. Level the mixture and cover with another baking paper.
10. Let cool for up to an hour then cut into small squares. The nougat can be kept in an airtight container.
11. To serve, beat the cream and incorporate the icing sugar. Top the nougat squares with the Chantilly, the washed redcurrants, raspberries and the mint leaves.

SERVES: **4** | PREP TIME: **10 MINS** | COOKING TIME: **45 MINS**

Melon Tiramisu

1 cantaloupe melon
10 finger biscuits
500 g / 1 lb 2 oz of mascarpone
350 ml / 12 fl. oz / 1 ½ cup of double (heavy) cream
200 g / 7 oz of fresh pineapple
150 g / 5 oz of caster (superfine) sugar
3 tbsp of grated coconut
120 ml / 4 fl. oz / ½ cup of coconut milk
1 tsp of cinnamon powder

1. Cut the melon in four, remove the skin and seeds and cut into thin strips.
2. Cut the pineapple into very small dices.
3. Whip the cream until stiff, then add the mascarpone, sugar and coconut milk and continue to whisk until the mixture is homogeneous (be careful not to overbeat).
4. Coarsely crush the finger biscuits, and arrange them in the bottom of a dish.
5. Sprinkle with coconut milk and a pinch of cinnamon.
6. Cover with half of the cream, then the melon and pineapple and the remaining cream.
7. Sprinkle with grated coconut and chill for at least 1 hour before serving.
8. Finish with cinnamon powder.

MAKES: **20** | PREP TIME: **10 HOURS** | COOKING TIME: **1 HOUR**

Fig and Almond Panetti

700 g / 1 lb 8 oz / 3 cups plain (all purpose) flour
700 g / 1 lb 8 oz / 3 cups honey
400 g / 13 oz / 2 cups dark chocolate
1 ½ tbsp cocoa powder
450 g / 1 lb / 2 cups peanuts
250 g / 9 oz / 1 cup almonds
200 g / 7 oz / 1 cup hazelnuts (cob nuts)
50 g / 2 oz of dried figs
120 ml / 4 fl. oz / ½ cup olive oil
1 tbsp black pepper
nutmeg, grated to taste

1. Pour the honey into a pan with the chocolate cut into pieces.
2. Dissolve the honey and chocolate over low heat, stirring occasionally.
3. Cut the figs into small pieces, hazelnuts and almonds in half and leave the whole peanuts.
4. Put the flour in a bowl, pour the melted chocolate and honey and mix. Pour the oil and mix again.
5. Add all the dried fruit, grated nutmeg, pepper and cocoa.
6. Mix all the ingredients by hand.
7. Make dough balls and place them carefully on the baking sheet, spaced enough from each other.
8. Rest for 10 hours if possible.
9. Cook the dough at 150°C / 300F / gas 2 for about one hour, checking fairly frequently.
10. Eat slightly warm.

MAKES: 40 | PREP TIME: 30 MINS | COOKING TIME: 20 MINS

Amaretti

225 g / 8 oz / 2 cups ground almonds

150 g / 5 oz / 1 cup sifted icing (confectioner's) sugar

1 egg white

1 to 2 tbsp almond extract

Blanched almonds for decoration (optional)

1. Preheat the oven to 180C (160C fan) / 350F / gas mark 4.
2. Grease 2 baking trays and cover with baking paper.
3. Whisk the egg white and almond extract in a bowl until frothy.
4. Put the ground almonds and icing sugar in a large bowl and make a well.
5. Add the egg white and mix with a metal spoon until the dough is a soft texture.
6. Form into balls about a teaspoon worth of dough and arrange on the baking sheets, spacing them well. They can be decorated with a blanched almond each.
7. Cook the biscuits for 15 to 20 minutes, they should be lightly browned.
8. Let them cool on a rack.

Chocolate and Chestnut Tiramisu

250 g / 9 oz of chestnut puree
6 glazed chestnuts
150 g of whipped cream
60 ml / 2 fl. oz / ¼ cup of matured whisky
200 g mascarpone
35 g of icing (confectioner's) sugar
1 egg
2 egg yolks
6 finger biscuits
20 g unsweetened cocoa

1. Whip the cream then gently fold in the chestnut puree.
2. Beat the mascarpone, 2 egg yolks and whole egg, then add the icing sugar.
3. Combine the two mixtures.
4. Soak the biscuits with the whisky, mixed with the cocoa.
5. Place the soaked crushed biscuits at the bottom of the serving dishes.
6. Top with the chestnut mixture.
7. Sprinkle with the glazed chestnuts.

Raspberry and Champagne Zabaglione

200 g / 7 oz / ¾ cup raspberries
180 g / 6 oz / 2 / 3 cup caster (superfine) sugar
400 ml / 13 fl. oz / 2 cups champagne
8 egg yolks
1 tsp vanilla extract
1 lemon, grated zest and juiced

1. Put the eggs in a saucepan. Place the saucepan over a water bath, on a medium heat.
2. Add the sugar, vanilla and lemon zest. Whisk until foamy and pale.
3. Put the saucepan into a water bath on medium heat.
4. Then stir in the champagne gradually while beating.
5. Puree the raspberries and filter to remove the pips.
6. Add to the mixture and fold gently.
7. Serve the warm zabaglione with almond biscuits or gingerbread.

SERVES: **6** | PREP TIME: **45 MINS** | COOKING TIME: **45 MINS**

Profiteroles

FOR THE CHOUX PASTRY
150 g / 5 oz / 1 cup plain (all purpose)
   flour
125 g / 4 ½ oz / ½ cup butter
4 eggs
1 tbsp sugar
2 pinches salt

FOR THE SAUCE
150 g / 5 oz / ½ cup dark chocolate
2 tbsp butter
1 tablespoon milk

FOR THE FILLING
250 ml / 8 fl. oz / 1 cup double
   (heavy) cream
25 g / 1 oz icing (confectioner's) sugar

1. Preheat the oven to 210°C / 420F / gas 7.
2. Heat the butter over low heat then add the sugar, salt and 250ml / 8 fl. oz /
   1 cup of water and whisk.
3. Remove from the heat and add the flour all at once, whisking. Return to
   the heat and cook, stirring quickly until the dough pulls away from pan.
4. Remove the pan from the heat and stir in the eggs one at a time, while
   still whisking.
5. Place the dough in a piping bag fitted with a plain tip and form small balls
   of dough on a baking sheet, spacing them well as they rise during cooking.
6. Bake for 30 minutes, leaving the oven door ajar to let the moisture escape.
7. Break the chocolate in a saucepan. Add the butter in pieces and milk.
   Melt over low heat, stirring until you obtain a sauce. Reserve in a water bath.
8. Beat the cream until stiff then incorporate the sugar and refrigerate.
9. Remove the choux from the oven and let cool.
10. Cut the choux three-quarters of their height. Fill each with a small scoop
    of whipped cream. Place the caps on top.
11. Place the choux in bowls and sprinkle with chocolate sauce. Serve immediately.

Index

THE ROAD

Wole Soyinka

THE ROAD

LONDON
Oxford University Press
IBADAN
1965

Oxford University Press, Amen House, London E.C.4

GLASGOW NEW YORK TORONTO MELBOURNE WELLINGTON
BOMBAY CALCUTTA MADRAS KARACHI LAHORE DACCA
CAPE TOWN SALISBURY NAIROBI IBADAN ACCRA
KUALA LUMPUR HONG KONG

PRINTED AND BOUND IN ENGLAND BY
HAZELL WATSON AND VINEY LTD
AYLESBURY, BUCKS

Characters

MURANO	*personal servant to Professor*
KOTONU	*driver, lately of 'No Danger No Delay'*
SAMSON	*passenger tout and driver's mate to*
	Kotonu
SALUBI	*driver-trainee*
PROFESSOR	*proprietor etc. of the drivers' haven.*
	Formerly Sunday-school teacher and
	lay-reader
CHIEF-IN-TOWN	*a politician*
SAY TOKYO KID	*driver and captain of thugs*
PARTICULARS JOE	*a policeman*
SEVERAL LAY-ABOUTS	
A CROWD	

Translations of the Yoruba songs and a glossary
of pidgin words will be found after p. 96

For the Producer

Since the mask-idiom employed in *The Road* will be strange to many, the preface poem Alagemo should be of help. Agemo is simply, a religious cult of flesh dissolution.

The dance is the movement of transition; it is used in the play as a visual suspension of death – in much the same way as Murano, the mute, is a dramatic embodiment of this suspension. He functions as an arrest of time, or death, since it was in his 'agemo' phase that the lorry knocked him down. Agemo, the mere phase, includes the passage of transition from the human to the divine essence (as in the festival of Ogun in this play), as much as the part psychic, part intellectual grope of Professor towards the essence of death.

Alagemo

I heard! I felt their reach
And heard my naming named.
The pit is there, the digger fell right through
My roots have come out in the other world.
Make away. Agemo's hoops
Are pathways of the sun.
Rain-reeds, unbend to me, Quench
The burn of cartwheels at my waist!
Pennant in the stream of time—Now,
Gone, and Here the Future
Make way. Let the rivers woo
The thinning, thinning Here and
Vanished Leap that was the Night
And the split that snatched the heavy-lidded
She-twin into Dawn.
No sweat-beads droop beneath
The plough-wings of the hawk.
No beetle finds a hole between Agemo's toes.
When the whirlwind claps his feet
It is the sundering of the . . . name no ills . . .
Of . . . the Not-to-be
Of the moistening moment of a breath . . .
Approach. Approach and feel
Did I not speak? Is there not flesh
Between the dead man's thumbs?

PART ONE

Dawn is barely breaking on a road-side shack, a ragged fence and a corner of a church with a closed stained-glass window. Above this a cross-surmounted steeple tapers out of sight. Thrusting downstage from a corner of the shack is the back of a 'bolekaja' (mammy waggon), lop-sided and minus its wheels. It bears the inscription—AKSIDENT STORE—ALL PART AVAILEBUL. In the opposite corner, a few benches and empty beer-cases used as stools. Downstage to one side, a table and chair, placed in contrasting tidiness.

Kotonu is asleep on a mat against the tailboard, Samson stretched a few feet away, a small bundle under his head. In the other corner the motor-park lay-abouts are sprawled on the floor and on benches, Salubi on two benches placed together, his driver's uniform neatly folded beside his head. Murano lies coiled under the Professor's table.

Murano gets up. Goes and washes his face from a pot just showing among rubble of worn tyres, hubs, twisted bumpers etc. Picks up his climbing rope, his gourd and his 'osuka' and sets off. Samson wakes half-way through his ablutions and watches him furtively. As Murano disappears he considers following him but thinks better of it, returns to his mat.

The tower clock strikes five. Samson stretches, tosses about restlessly. Eventually he gets up, scratching. Goes outside and tries to follow Murano with his eyes. Gives up. He ambles around aimlessly, stopping to pick up crumbs from a plate lying on a table. Then he goes out and urinates against the wall, stretching like a practised idler. About to re-enter, a thought strikes him and he turns and with some trepidation, goes towards the churchyard. Goes through a gap in the fence, and eggs himself further and further inside. Startling him, the tower clock strikes the half-hour and he belts back, flinging himself through the gap before he realizes what the noise is. Shakes his fist at the tower and returns to the shack.

He sees all the others sleeping peacefully and this incenses him. Gives Salubi a kick in the leg but Salubi only draws it back on the bench. He pushes another off the bench. The man continues his sleep on the floor. All round them are the empty cups used at the last carousing; Samson picks up a tin mug, flings it up in the air and lets it drop. Only one or two react, but this does not go beyond turning on the other side. Disgusted he goes over to a spider's web in the corner, pokes it with a stick. He soon wearies of this.

In frustration, Samson flings himself on the mat only to be flung up again by the clock suddenly striking the hour.

Salubi stirs, gets up.

SALUBI: Six o'clock I bet. I don't know how it is, but no matter when I go to sleep, I wake up when it strikes six. Now that is a miracle.

[*He gets out his chewing stick, begins to chew on it.*]

SAMSON: There is a miracle somewhere but not what you say. Maybe the sight of you using a chewing stick.

SALUBI: Look Samson, it's early in the morning. Go back to sleep if you're going to start that again.

[*He starts to put on his chauffeur's uniform.*]

SAMSON: Who lend you uniform?

SALUBI: I buy it with my own money.

[*Samson goes over, feels the cloth.*]

SAMSON: Second-hand.

SALUBI: So what?

SAMSON: At least you might have washed it. Look at that blood-stain—has someone been smashing your teeth?

SALUBI: Rubbish. Na palm-oil.

SAMSON: All right all right. But you are a funny person. Funny

like one of those street idiots. How can anyone buy a
uniform when he hasn't got a job?

SALUBI: Impression. I take uniform impress all future employer.

SAMSON: With that smear on the front?

SALUBI: Go mind your own business you jobless tout.

SAMSON: Me a jobless tout? May I ask what you are?

SALUBI: A uniformed private driver—temporary unemploy.
[*Straightens his outfit.*]

SAMSON: God almighty! You dey like monkey wey stoway
inside sailor suit.

SALUBI: Na common jealousy dey do you. I know I no get job,
but I get uniform.
[*Starts to shine his brass buttons.*]

SAMSON [*shakes his head.*]: Instead of using all that labour to
shine your buttons you should spare some for your teeth,
you know, and your body—a little soap and sponge would
do it. After all, new uniform deserves new body. White
coat deserves white teeth.

SALUBI [*desperately.*]: Wes matter? Na me you take dream last
night or na wetin? Why you no mind your own business
for heaven's sake!

SAMSON: Because I have no business to mind you dirty pig. Why
am I sitting here at this time of the morning? Every
self-respecting tout is already in the motor park badgering
passengers. Look at all these touts still sleeping. They have
no pride in their job. Part-time tout part-time burglar. In
any case they are the pestilence of the trade. No professional
dignity. Hear them snoring as if their exhaust has dropped
off. Now that is what Kotonu expects me to do—start
touting for any lorry which happens to come along. Is that
the sort of life for the Champion Tout of Motor Parks?

SALUBI: I think say beggar no get choice.

SAMSON: Is that so? Of course you should know. You are ready to crawl on your belly and beg for anything. As for me, I am a proud man. I tout for my own driver, not for anyone else. I'm a one-driver tout, no more no less.

SALUBI: You say you get pride and still yet you are a conductor on bolekaja.

SAMSON: Nonsense, we run a bus. The seats face where you are going, just like the driver himself and the first-class passengers. In a common bolekaja you turn your side or your back to where you are going.

SALUBI: Anyway, the matter is that you are going with passenger lorry. You and these ruffians, you are the same. Me, I don't drive lorry. I drive only private owner—no more no less.

SAMSON: Private wey no get licence. Go siddon my friend.
[*Salubi gives the last button a flourish, straightens himself and looks satisfied.*]

SALUBI: As I am standing so, I fit to drive the Queen of England.

SAMSON: One look at you and she will abdicate.

SALUBI: All I need now is a licence. It is only a matter of getting Professor to forge one for me.

SAMSON: Ask him.

SALUBI: I have asked him a hundred times, but he always says . . .

SAMSON [*mimicking.*]: Go away. Come back when you have a job.

SALUBI: You see. And a man can't get a job without a licence.

SAMSON: And you can't get a licence without a job. So why don't you just go and hang yourself.

SALUBI: I no sabbe do am. You fit show me?

SAMSON: When Professor returns and I will tell him you tried to hang yourself.

SALUBI [*jumping.*]: You can't frighten me you hear. Who do you think is afraid of that madman. [*Looking towards the churchyard.*] I wonder if he is still asleep.

[*Progressively during the scene, the sleeping forms get up, give their faces a wash, go round the back-yard, hang on the fence etc.*]

SAMSON: If he ever sleeps. I cannot understand the man, going to sleep in the churchyard with all that dead-body.

SALUBI: That is how to make money you know. If you make abracadabra with spirits you can get money from them.

SAMSON: You think Professor has money?

SALUBI: The man too clever. One of these days I will find out where he hides his money. He may even be millionaire.

SAMSON [*wistfully.*]: Sometimes I think, what will I do with all that money if I am a millionaire?

SALUBI: First I will marry ten wives.

SAMSON: Why ten?

SALUBI: I no fit count pass ten.

SAMSON: Just like you to waste money on women.

SALUBI: Why not? What else can a man do with a million pounds?

SAMSON: Me, I will buy all the transport lorries in the country, then make Kotonu the head driver.

SALUBI: Kotonu? Who be Kotonu? He get experience pass me?

SAMSON: You? Don't make me laugh. You are not fit to wipe the cow-dung from his tyres. You I will make my private driver—and if you come near me with a dirty uniform like that, I will have you thrashed like a horse.

SALUBI: Who get dirty uniform? I wash am starch am yesterday. Abi three pence starch no fit stiff am one day?

SAMSON: As for Professor, I will give him special office with air-conditioner, automatic printing press and so on and so forth, so he can forge driving licences for all my drivers. The man is an artist and, as a millionaire, I must support culture.

SALUBI: The day the police catch you ...

SAMSON: Which kind police? They will form line in front of my house every morning to receive their tip. No one will touch my lorry on the road.

[*He lifts the Professor's chair, dumps it on the big table and climbs on to it, leaps down almost immediately and whips the coverlet off Kotonu who stirs and slowly wakes up later. Wraps the coverlet around his shoulders and climbs back on the table. Takes out the Professor's glasses and wears them low on his nose. Puts on an imposing look and surveys a line in front of him with scorn. Breaks into a satisfied grin.*]

SAMSON: E sa mi.

SALUBI [*down on his knees, salaams.*]: African millionaire!

SAMSON: I can't hear you.

SALUBI: Delicate millionaire!

SAMSON: Wes matter? You no chop this morning? I say I no hear you.

SALUBI: Samson de millionaire!

SAMSON: Ah, my friends, what can I do for you?

SALUBI [*in attitude of prayer.*]: Give us this day our daily bribe. Amen.

SAMSON [*dips in an imaginary purse, he is about to fling to them a fistful of coins when he checks his hand.*]: Now remember, officers first. Superintendents! [*Flings the coins. Salubi scrambles and picks up the money.*] Inspectors! [*Action is repeated.*] Sergeants! [*Again Salubi grabs the coins.*] Now that is what I call a well disciplined force. Next, those with one or two stripes. [*Flings out more money. Salubi retreating to a new position, picks up the largesse.*] Excellent! Excellent! And now, those who are new to the game. [*Same action.*] You may go now. And good hunting friends. [*He and Salubi collapse laughing. Kotonu has sat up watching.*]

SALUBI: Haba, make man talk true, man wey get money get power.

SAMSON: God I go chop life make I tell true. I go chop the life

so tey God go jealous me. And if he take jealousy kill me I
will go start bus service between heaven and hell.

SALUBI: Which kin' bus for heaven? Sometimes na aeroplane or
helicopter den go take travel for Paradise.

SAMSON [*reverting to his role.*]: Come here.

SALUBI: Yessssssssah.

SAMSON: Have you had a wash today?

SALUBI: Myself sah?

SAMSON: Open your mouth . . . go on, open your mouth.
Wider! It stinks.

SALUBI: Sah?

SAMSON: It stinks. It stinks so much that I will promote you
Captain of my private bodyguard. When the police bring
their riot squad with tear-gas and all that nonsense, you
will open your mouth and breathe on them. That is what
is known as counter-blast.

SALUBI: Yesssssssah.

SAMSON: But you must take care not to breathe in my direction.
A compost heap has its own uses, as long as the wind is
blowing in the other direction. There have been times
when you actually dared to breathe in my face.

SALUBI: Me sah? To breathe into millionaire face. My very self
sah?

SAMSON: Your very self ma? Do you accuse me of lying?

SALUBI: I sorry too much sah.

SAMSON: And your driving is becoming a menace. You drivers
are all the same. When you get on an endless
stretch of road your buttocks open wide and you begin to
fart on passengers in the first-class compartment. Is that
right?

SALUBI: Yesssssssah. I mean no sah. At all at all sah.

SAMSON: Now I want you to take the car—the long one—and
drive along the Marina at two o'clock. All the fine fine

girls just coming from offices, the young and tender faces fresh from school—give them lift to my house. Old bones like me must put fresh tonic in his blood.

[*Busy with laughter, they do not see the Professor approach. Salubi is the first to see him, he stands petrified for some moments, then begins to stutter.*]

SALUBI: Samson ... Professor ... !

SAMSON: What about him?

[*Salubi, with trembling finger, points in his direction, but Samson refuses to turn round.*]

You think you have seen a new-born fool do you? What would Professor be doing here at this time of the day?

[*As Professor gets to the door, Salubi dives under the table. Samson, too late, turns round and stares petrified.*

Professor is a tall figure in Victorian outfit—tails, top-hat etc., all thread-bare and shiny at the lapels from much ironing. He carries four enormous bundles of newspaper and a fifth of paper odds and ends impaled on a metal rod stuck in a wooden rest. A chair-stick hangs from one elbow, and the other arm clutches a road-sign bearing a squiggle and the one word, 'BEND'.]

PROF. [*he enters in a high state of excitement, muttering to himself.*]: Almost a miracle ... dawn provides the greatest miracles but this ... in this dawn has exceeded its promise. In the strangest of places. ... God God God but there is a mystery in everything. A new discovery every hour—I am used to that, but that I should be led to where this was hidden, sprouted in secret for heaven knows how long ... for there was no doubt about it, this word was growing, it was growing from earth until I plucked it. ...

[*He has reached the place where his table normally is. Puzzled, he looks round, but does not see Samson perched above him.*]

But is this my station? I could have sworn ...

[*Suddenly suspicious, he clutches the road-sign possessively.*]

If this is a trick I swear they shan't take it from me. If my eyes were deluded and my body led here by spells I shall not surrender the fruit of my vigil. No one can take it from me!

[*He looks up at last, sees Samson, scrutinizes him carefully.*]

You sir, are not one of my habituals, or I would know you.

SAMSON: N-n-n-no.

PROF.: So, you admit it, and it is no use pretending you are.

SAMSON: No . . . I mean . . .

[*Looking down suddenly, Professor sees Salubi's rear protruding from under the table. He strikes a defensive position, brandishes the chair-stick and jabs him again and again.*]

PROF.: Come out of there. I can see you. How many of you are there? Come out come out. You may be the devil's own army but my arm is powered with the unbroken Word!

SAMSON: P-p-please sir, I think you have made a mistake.

PROF.: I have?

SAMSON: Perhaps you missed your way.

PROF.: You think I did? Indeed anything is possible when I pursue the Word. But . . . and mind you tell the truth . . . you are not here to take the Word from me?

SAMSON: Oh no . . . not at all. You must have missed your way that's all.

PROF.: Then I must hurry. [*Turns to go, stops.*] But first, can you tell me where I am?

SAMSON: Oh yes. In the wrong place.

PROF.: Ah. I thought so. Strange that I should find myself here. I was drawn perhaps by some sympathy of spirit. Do you happen to follow the path yourself?

SAMSON: What path? I mean . . . no . . . aren't you in a hurry? Good-bye.

PROF. [*surveys his height with new wonder.*]: Yes, you seem a knowing man, cutting yourself from common touch with

earth. But that is a path away from all true communion ...
the Word is not to be found in denial.

SAMSON: I agree ... please go now, we are rather busy.

PROF.: May I ask who you are? I am, I confess, a little dazed by
my error, but I have vague recollection of your face. ...

SAMSON: Not in the least. I am sure we have never met before.

PROF.: You live here?

SAMSON: Yes ... er ... I own the place. In fact, I am a
millionaire.

PROF.: You are what?

SAMSON [*gaining courage.*]: Yes, that's right. A millionaire.

PROF.: I am so confused, but I have sight and vision only for the
Word and it may chance, sometimes, that I miss my way
among worldly humans. [*Going.*]

SAMSON: That is what I have been trying to tell you. Good-bye.

PROF. [*shaking his head sadly.*]: Such dangers beset us who seek
after the Word. [*He sees Kotonu sitting up, stops.*] But I do
know *you.* You are the coast-to-coast driver who gave up
the road.

SAMSON: Did he? I mean who? Oh him. Why, I employed
him only this morning. He must have changed his mind.

PROF.: Aha, did I not say that I was drawn here on a wave of
sympathy? I knew I could not miss my way without
reason.

[*Samson signals Kotonu frantically to get Professor out.*]

KOTONU: If you like Professor, I will come home with you.

PROF.: But your employer ...?

SAMSON: ... has no objection at all. Take him. In fact I no
longer need him. He dreams too much. Go on, you are
sacked. Good-bye to both of you. Good-bye ...
good-bye.

PROF.: Come then, I have a new wonder to show you ... a
madness where a motor-car throws itself against a tree—

Gbram! And showers of crystal flying on broken souls.

SAMSON [*suddenly alarmed.*]: Wait! What was that about an accident?

PROF.: Are you that ignorant of the true path to the Word. It is never an accident.

SAMSON: Well call it what you will. But you are not taking him to see that sort of rubbish.

PROF. [*bristling.*]: How dare you? Do you take me for a common gawper after misery?

SALUBI [*from beneath.*]: Samson are you mad? For God's sake let them go.

PROF. [*to Kotonu.*]: This millionaire—did he purchase your soul too?

KOTONU: Pay no attention Professor, let's go.

SAMSON [*almost plaintive.*]: Kotonu don't go with him.

[*Professor approaches him.*]

SALUBI: Now he is going to find us out you stupid tout.

PROF.: My bed is among the dead, and when the road raises a victory cry to break my sleep I hurry to a disgruntled swarm of souls full of spite for their rejected bodies. It is a market of stale meat, noisy with flies and quarrelsome with old women. The place I speak of is not far from here, if you wish to come . . . you shall be shown this truth of my endeavours—

SAMSON: No thank you very much. I don't willingly seek out unpleasant sights.

PROF.: You are afraid? There are dangers in the Quest I know, but the Word may be found companion not to life, but Death. Three souls you know, fled up that tree. You would think, to see it, that the motor-car had tried to clamber after them. Oh there was such an angry buzz but the matter was beyond repair. They died, all three of them crucified on rigid branches. I found this word growing

where their blood had spread and sunk along plough
scouring of the wheel. Now tell me you who sit above it
all, do you think my sleep was broken over nothing, over
a meaningless event?

SALUBI: Don't answer him Samson. Just let him go.

SAMSON: But there is no need to take Kotonu to see it.

SALUBI: Let him go before it is too late.

KOTONU: Let's go Professor. [*He ushers Professor towards the
door, turns back to Samson.*] It is only a business trip. Stop
fidgetting. [*They go.*]

PROF.: But you must not think I accept all such manifestations
as truth. It may be a blind. I know this is not the Word, but
every discovery is a sign-post . . . eventually the revelation
will stand naked, unashamed . . . the subterfuge will be
over, my cause vindicated. . . .

[*His voice trails off in the distance. Samson and Salubi remain
motionless until they can no longer hear him.*]

SALUBI [*crawls out and dusts himself.*]: All I can say is, you have
the luck of a hunter's dog. I mean, if ever a thief more
than deserved to be caught red-handed. . . .

SAMSON: But what did Kotonu mean by that?

SALUBI: What?

SAMSON: He said he was going on a business trip. This is a funny
way to talk about a thing like that.

SALUBI: But he was going on a business trip.

SAMSON: What business trip?

SALUBI: Get out. You are his mate aren't you? Do you want to
pretend you don't know?

SAMSON: What don't I know?

SALUBI: Well where do you think I get this uniform?

SAMSON: Stole it of course. It's just like you to rob a dead man.
Common shop-lifter. When Sergeant Burma was alive
you wouldn't dare.

SALUBI: I am glad you can joke about it. Because I bought it from your mate.

SAMSON: From Kotonu? Are you gone mad?

SALUBI: Why don't you open your eyes and see who is now operating behind that tailboard?

SAMSON: And who will I find? Your father's decomposing corpse?

SALUBI: If he's there then your friend must have put him there for sale?

SAMSON: You are a liar!

SALUBI: You wait. When he returns you will see for yourself.

SAMSON: Don't talk rubbish. That was Sergeant Burma's department.

SALUBI: Sergeant Burma is dead.

SAMSON: And when did Kotonu become his business partner?

SALUBI: Not partner friend, successor. Kotonu has taken over.

SAMSON [*wildly*.]: Liar! You're just a dirty back-biter.

SALUBI: I am saying nothing. You'll see for yourself.

SAMSON: When? When? How could it happen and I not know about it?

SALUBI: Where do you hide your eyes? Look, better get down before you continue to deceive yourself. If Professor stumbles in here again he won't be so blind this time.

SAMSON [*getting down slowly*.]: Oh God. Oh God. I don't believe it. But what is Kotonu trying to do? Is he pretending he doesn't care?

SALUBI: Look, just put this back before the old man returns. He can't make the same mistake twice.

[*They re-arrange the table.*]

SAMSON: He won't come back. A mistake like that always scares him. He thinks it proves that he has gone deeply wrong somewhere. You'll see. When he comes in the afternoon we will hear all about it.

SALUBI: I still think you are a lucky man. Any moment I
    expected him to knock you off the table with that word
    business.

SAMSON: But Kotonu is not like that. What is he trying to do?
    This isn't necessary at all. I only said take back your licence,
    not start keeping shop for the mortuary.

SALUBI: Well you wanted him back on the road didn't you? So
    now he's back full blast. General trader and—perhaps
    occasional supplier too.

SAMSON: So you're taking your evil mouth curse him are you?
    It's your head will supply that kind of goods you chronic
    accident of a driver!
    [*Sits down dejected.*]

SALUBI: You are not yet thankful for your escape. You've gone
    and sat in Professor's chair again.

SAMSON: Right now I don't care. Kotonu has gone with him
    and I bet he comes back worse than ever.

SALUBI[*going.*]: Why you no surrender self? The man say 'e no
    want drive again but you continue worry am as if you na
    in wife. Haba! Abi when den born am dem tie steering
    wheel for in neck?

SAMSON: This is all Professor's doing. And it was on him I was
    pinning my hopes, I was thinking he might be able to
    reform this runaway mate of mine. Now he goes and
    shows him yet another crash.

SALUBI: He's mad. Why you dey worry your head for dat kind
    person? Abi you tink say Kotonu no sabbe de man dey
    craze.

    [*The window the the church is thrown open suddenly,
    revealing the lectern, a bronze eagle on whose outstretched
    wings rests a huge tome. Shortly afterwards music from the
    organ billows out towards the shack. Samson listens for some
    time.*]

SAMSON: He's not as good as the first man—that's what
   Professor says.

SALUBI: Why he dey come play dat ting every morning self?
   Nobody dey inside church.

SAMSON: Rehearsal stupid. You think people just sit down in
   front of the organ and play just like that? Ah, when
   Professor was Professor, he would go up after the service
   and correct the organist where he went wrong. And even
   during the singing if he heard a wrong note he would shake
   his head and look round the church making tch-tch-tch-
   tch-tch. Every time the organist saw that, he knew he was
   in serious trouble.

SALUBI: Why 'e no kuku play the ting inself?

SAMSON: Where were you born that you don't know about
   Professor?

SALUBI: I only know there was the matter of church funds?
   Did he go to prison?

SAMSON: You think they just put somebody in prison like that?
   Professor his very self? Of course you don't know your
   history. When Professor entered church, everybody turned
   round and the eyes of the congregation followed him to
   his pew—and he had his own private pew let me tell you,
   and if a stranger went and sat in it, the church warden
   wasted no time driving him out.

SALUBI: Dat one no to church, na high society.

SAMSON: You no sabbe de ting wey man dey call class so shurrup
   your mout. Professor enh, he get class. He get style. That
   suit he wears now, that was the very way he used to dress
   to evening service. I tell you, the whole neighbourhood
   used to come and watch him, they would gather in this
   very bar and watch him through the windows, him and his
   hundred handkerchiefs spread out on the pew in front of
   him. . . . [*Samson has begun to act Professor, spreading out a*

*few greasecloths and rags on a bench and kneeling behind them.
He is a meticulous fop in demeanour. Suddenly he rises, makes
a formal bow.*] That bow, it means that the preacher has
just mentioned the name of Jesus Christ. And let me tell
you enh, the preacher directed his sermon to Professor for
approval. [*He sits, listening attentively. Suddenly he frowns,
takes a notebook from his books and writes in it.*] That means a
point of controversy, to be hotly debated after church.
[*Dabs his brows gently and gravely lays the handkerchief aside.*]
He never used a handkerchief twice. Never.

SALUBI: What about the day they said he fought with the
bishop?

SAMSON: Which kind of fighting?

SALUBI: Didn't he slap the bishop?

SAMSON: I don't think you understand anything I've been
telling you. You think Professor could ever descend to
such bushman taxi-driver stuff? My friend, they did have
a fight but it was a duel of gentlemen. Look, I'll tell you
what happened. Just because the bishop thought he had
B.A., B.D. . . .

SALUBI: How much?

SAMSON: B.D. Bachelor of Divinity stupid. But B.D. or no
B.D. the man just couldn't knack oratory like the Professor.
In fact everybody always said that Professor ought to
preach the sermons but a joke is a joke, I mean, the man is
not ordained. So we had to be satisfied with him reading
the lesson and I'm telling you, three-quarters of the
congregation only came to hear his voice. And the bishop
was jealous. When the bishop came on his monthly visit
and preached the sermon after Professor's lesson, it was a
knock-out pure and simple. Before bishop open in mout' half
de church done go sleep. And the ones who stayed
awake only watched Professor taking notes. [*Whips*

out his notebook and stabs it with furious notes.] That means, serious grammatical error. Bishop done trow bomb!

SALUBI: En-hen. If na you be bishop and somebody dey do dat kin' ting you no go vex?

SAMSON: Wait small you no hear de proper fight yet. That was the day the wall of Jericho (*he points*) fell down. The bishop thought he would teach Professor a lesson. So during sermon, he began to use Jesus Christ every other sentence. At first Professor tried to keep it up. [*He rises, bowing and sitting and bowing and sitting, more and more rapidly without however losing his elegance and general fastidiousness, discarding one handkerchief after the other.*] I was there. So was Kotonu. The usual crowd was here too but we all got so excited that we ran from here and climbed the wall to see better. We wanted to see which of them would win, whether Professor would get cramp for in neck or the bishop would run out of grammar. [*The organ music carries on the conflict in tone and pace.*] The congregation was very silent, they knew what was happening and they knew this was the final duel between their bishop and their lay-reader. . . . [*Samson makes a sudden sharp bow, and remains there for some moments. When he speaks he still retains the position.*] That was how Professor solved it. He made one more bow and he stuck there. The bishop sermonized his head off, the church shook with reverberations from passionate grammar but na so Professor bend in head —'e no move one inch. [*Samson sits, shaking his head in remembered admiration.*]

SALUBI: But how wall come fall down?

SAMSON: That was our fault. We were riding the wall like a victory horse—everybody. Grown-up customers and all the riff-raff, turning somersaults in and out of the churchyard. Suddenly—Gbram!

SALUBI: With you on top?

SAMSON: You no fit tell man from rubble I tell you. The whole church rushed out but there was no need. Nobody was injured. You can imagine, everybody running out just when the bishop was shaking the pulpit and blasting humanity to hell. That is why the wall was not re-built, the bishop forbade it. Sheer spitefulness I call that.

SALUBI: What time he tief the church funds then?

SAMSON: He didn't steal anything.

SALUBI [*shrugs.*]: One of these days I will find out where he hides the money.

SAMSON: You try. Professor will cockroach you like an old newspaper.

SALUBI: You tink I fear all dat in nonsense?

SAMSON [*wistfully.*]: The parish was really hot soup in those days. Politics no get dramatic pass am.

SALUBI: Me a dey go find work. De whole morning done vanish for your cinema show.

SAMSON: Where you dey run go self? Siddon here make we talk.

SALUBI: Not me. If I find lorry wey want experienced tout I go come call you.

SAMSON: Who beg you? Commot my friend.

SALUBI: Okay. Siddon here dey make cinema. [*Goes.*]

SAMSON [*ambles restlessly round the room.*]: A fine shape I am in when I actually want that stink-bug to stay and keep me company. Ogiri mouth. [*He grows more and more dejected.*] If he gets a job before Kotonu puts us back on the road the man will become simply intolerable. All the fault of that Kotonu. What use am I, a tout without his driver. I should have known it would come sooner or later. He's never acted like a normal person. When other drivers go out of the way to kill a dog, Kotonu nearly somersaults the lorry trying to avoid a flea-racked mongrel. Why, I ask him, why? Don't you know a dog is Ogun's meat? Take warning Kotonu. Before it's too late take warning and kill us a dog.

[*As his grumbling gets in stride, Kotonu returns with an armful of motor parts, an old shoe, a cap etc. Goes into the mammy-waggon stall through hidden entrance up-stage. He can be heard occasionally but he tries to move silently. Occasionally he lifts up the top-half tarpaulin covering and pushes out an object, trying to remain unobserved by Samson. Half-way through Samson's moaning, one of the lay-abouts strums his guitar, begins to sing*]:

> Ona orun jin o eeeee
> Ona orun jin dereba rora
> E e dereba rora
> E e dereba rora
> Ona orun jin o eeeee
> Eleda mi ma ma buru
> Esin baba Bandele je l'odan
> Won o gbefun o
> Eleda mi ma ma buru
> Esin baba Bandele je l'odan
> Won o gbefun o[1]

[*The others hanging by the fence join in idly. Samson turns angrily on the leader.*]

SAMSON: Get out get out. Is that the kind of song to be singing at this time of the morning? Why don't you go and look for work?

[*As if accustomed to this kind of outburst, the man waves Samson off, goes out. Samson turns, sees Kotonu who has finished in the stall and is now stretched full-length on the bench.*]

I didn't see you come back.

[1] See p. 100 for English translation.

KOTONU: You were talking to yourself when I came.

SAMSON: Did you hear what I said? I hope you did because it's all true so I hope you heard every word of it. Where is Professor?

KOTONU [*following his time-table.*]: Wandering over empty streets picking up his dirty bits of printed matter.

SAMSON: He is not likely to come back is he?

KOTONU: No. That business here has unsettled him. He is still trying to work out a meaning—you're lucky he didn't suspect you.

SAMSON: Didn't you bring anything back from the wreck?

KOTONU: What do you mean?

SAMSON: Don't think I don't know. You have been taking over Sergeant Burma's business.

KOTONU: Who told you?

SAMSON: Never mind. But I never thought it was like you somehow. After all, what excuse have you? You haven't been to war. You cannot pretend to be an out-and-out cannibal like Sergeant Burma.

KOTONU: A man gets tired of feeling too much.

[*Outside, the gang resume their song, singing the lewd verse now.*]

> Bebe yi ga e-e-e
> Bebe yi ga sisi je nda mi'ra
> E e sisi je nda mi'ra
> E e sisi je nda mi'ra
> Bebe yi ga, o po o
> Omi tide pe mi l'okobo Mo yo
> Sibesibe me le f'asape laya o
> Won ndi bebe leko o won ndi bebe
> Eko mo roye o, ah mama
> Eko lawo ya o egungun d'enia

[*Interspersed with salutations called out to passing friends and abusive comments on favourite targets.*]

KOTONU: Where is Zorro who never returned from the North without a basket of guinea-fowl eggs? Where is Akanni the Lizard? I have not seen any other tout who would stand on the lorry's roof and play the samba at sixty miles an hour. Where is Sigidi Ope? Where is Sapele Joe who took on six policemen at the crossing and knocked them all into the river?

SAMSON: Overshot the pontoon, went down with his lorry.

KOTONU: And Saidu-Say? Indian Charlie who taught us driving? Well, tried to teach you anyway and wore out his soul in the attempt. Where is Humphrey Bogart? Cimarron Kid? Have you known any other driver take an oil-tanker from Port Harcourt to Kaduna non-stop since Muftau died? Where is Sergeant Burma who treated his tanker like a child's toy?

SAMSON: Just the same. . . .

KOTONU: Sergeant Burma was never moved by these accidents. He told me himself how once he was stripping down a crash and found that the driver was an old comrade from the front. He took him to the mortuary but first he stopped to remove all the tyres.

SAMSON: He wasn't human.

KOTONU: But he was. He was. A man must protect himself against the indifference of comrades who desert him. Not to mention the hundred travellers whom you never really see until their faces are wiped clean by silence.

SAMSON: I see them. I am in the back with them and I see them. I talk to them and I abuse their grandfathers. But I don't carry on like you do.

KOTONU: You know, Professor is a bit like Sergeant Burma. He was moving round those corpses as if they didn't exist. All he cared about was re-planting that sign-post. To see him you would think he was Adam replanting the Tree of Life.

SAMSON: All right thank you. I don't want to hear any more.
[*Kotonu slides back into his favourite position, lying by the wall
of the store or sitting up against it. Most of the time he is half-
asleep, indifferent to what goes on around him. Enter Chief-in-
Town, a politician.*]

CHIEF-IN-TOWN: Captain!

SAMSON [*without turning round.*]: They've all gone.

CHIEF: Which motor-park?

SAMSON: Who knows? Anywhere they find a picking.

CHIEF: How long ago did they leave? I said I might need them
this morning.

SAMSON: No idea.

CHIEF: You are new around here. Are you . . . one of the boys?

SAMSON: I won't thug for you if that is what you mean.

CHIEF: You will, you will . . . just give yourself a few more days
sitting doing nothing. What about your friend?

SAMSON: He used to be my driver and I his tout. Now he doesn't
want any part of the road—except what is left of the sacrifice.

CHIEF: Sacrifice? What sacrifice?

SAMSON: Never mind. He doesn't thug either, and that is all
you really want to know.
[*Enter Say Tokyo Kid with a leap over the fence.*]

SAY T.: Chief-in-Town!

CHIEF: The Captain!

SAY T.: Chief-in-Town.

CHIEF: Say Tokyo Kid!

SAY T.: No dirty timber, thas me Chief.

CHIEF: How is the timber world?

SAY T.: Life is full of borers Chief. I feel them in my tummy.
Chief-in-Town! I was already on ma way to the moror
park when your car passed me. I shoured but you didn't
hear nuthin.

CHIEF: I need ten men.

SAY T.: Today?

CHIEF: This moment. Didn't you get my message?

SAY T.: No.

CHIEF: I sent my driver. He said he gave it to an old man in a black tuxedo.

SAY T: That would be Professor. He don't like us doing this kinra job. Well what's cooking Chief? Campaign.

CHIEF: No. Just a party meeting.

SAY T.: Oh. Are we for the general party or . . .

CHIEF: You know me, Personal Bodyguard.

SAY T:. Chief-in-Town!

CHIEF: How soon can you round them up?

SAY T.: Ten minutes, fifteen minutes—no more.

CHIEF: I want the toughest you can find. This meeting is going to be hot.

SAY T.: You know you can count on me Chief. What about . . .?

CHIEF: Stuff?

SAY T.: Yeah Chief. Yougot the old Chacha-Mu-Chacha?

[*Chief-in-Town takes out a small packet. Say Tokyo snatches it greedily.*]

SAY T. [*examines it, sniffs it.*]: Stuff Chief. Real stuff.

CHIEF: I will send the Land-Rover to the motor park.

SAY T.: No Chief. Send it here. I'll send round the word.

CHIEF: Don't fail me. Fifteen minutes.

SAY T.: Chief-in-Town!

[*Chief-in-Town goes. Say Tokyo quickly rolls himself a stick of hemp, sits in a corner and starts to inhale.*
Samson breaks from a corner where he has been poking the spider with a stick.]

SAMSON: You know, you remind me of a spider.

KOTONU: Why?

SAMSON: Yes, that's it. You are living just like a spider. This is your brother in this corner.

KOTONU: What are you getting at now?

SAMSON [*peering.*]: Facially, it even resembles you.

KOTONU: But I haven't got so many legs.

SAMSON: Who told you? Four rear tyres, two front and two spare. That is eight altogether. But you prefer to lie there and vegetate.

KOTONU [*irritably.*]: I knew it would be something like that. Why won't you give up?

SAMSON: Anyway, when you get tired of being a trader in dead lorries Chief-in-Town can take you up as a thug.

KOTONU: It isn't such a bad idea. At least I will see a man's face before I bash it in. Driving doesn't guarantee you that.
[*Say Tokyo Kid, his eyes fixed and glazed, achieves the 'state'. He seizes the big drum and goes out to the fence. Beats out the summons for his gang and returns to the shack while the echoes carry on. He sets about rolling more of the sticks for his gang who roll in one by one. Samson moves beside Kotonu, watching. They sit round the table, dragging on the hemp.
Through the door a uniformed policeman, Particulars Joe, thrusts his head through the door and sniffs the air, turns outside to look up and down the road and slides into the room. Barks suddenly.*]

PARTICULARS JOE: Wey your particulars?

A THUG: Particulars Joe!

PARTICULARS JOE: I say gimme your particulars.
[*Say Tokyo reaches out a stick of weed to him which he accepts behind his back. Darts back to the door and sits apart sniffing the weed. He gives a quick nod of appreciation to Say Tokyo who graciously waves it aside. One of his thugs picks up drum and taps out a slow rhythm. Say Tokyo, his eye shining madly, leaps up. Lights up Joe's cigarette.
Say Tokyo slowly flexes his arm muscles, looking from one arm to the other, luxuriating in the feel of his strength.*]

PARTICULARS JOE: Say Tokyo Kid!

SAY T.: I'm all right boy.

PARTICULARS JOE: No dirty timber.

SAY T.: No borer in re ol bole.

SAMSON: Oh what wouldn't I give for Professor to enter now.

SAY T. [*spits*.]: That's what would happen if your Professor came in. I don give a damn for that crazy guy and he know it. He's an awright guy but he sure act crazy sometimes and I'm telling you, one of these days, he's gonna go too far.

A THUG: The Captain!

SAY T.: I'm Say Tokyo Kid and I don't fear no son of man.

SAMSON: Yes you can talk now. But you run here fast enough to guzzle his wine.

SAY T.: So what? So long his guy keeps bringing that swell froth on every gourd, I'm gonna come here to pay ma respects. But a don' go for no ceremony abour' it. A don't mind his crazy talk, but all the rest of it, man, it ain't for Say Tokyo Kid.

PARTICULARS JOE [*somewhat dizzily*.]: Say Tokyo.

SAY T.: Thas me officer.

[*Particulars Joe gets groggier and groggier as the scene progresses, swaying more and more until by the end of the dance he is clutching his stomach and slithers to the ground.*]

PARTICULARS JOE: Gedu!

SAY T.: Thas me boy.

PARTICULARS JOE: No dirty timber:

SAY T.: Thas me kid.

PARTICULARS JOE: Igi dongboro lehin were!

SAY T.: Yio ba baba e.

PARTICULARS JOE: Gbegi ma gbe'yawo!

SAY T.: Yio ba 'ponri iya a'laiya e.

PARTICULARS JOE. Olomokuiya. [*Say Tokyo grins, both hands held in an insulting gesture.*]

SAY T.: I mean, a man has gotta have his pride. I don't carry no timber that ain't one hundred per cent. fit. I'm a guy of principles. Carrying timber ain't the same as carrying passengers I tell you. You carry any kind of guy. You take any kind of load. You carrying rubbish. You carrying lepers. The women tell you to stop because they's feeling the call of nature. If you don't stop they pee in your lorry. And whether you stop or not their chirren mess the place all over. The whole of the lorry is stinking from rotting food and all kinda refuse. That's a passenger lorry.

SALUBI: Say Tokyo Kid!

SAY T.: Thas me boy. No time for nonsense!

SAMSON: I don't know. I like to deal with people. Just think, carrying a dead load like that from one end of the world to another ...

SAY T.: Dead! You think a guy of timber is dead load. What you talking kid? You reckon you can handle a timber lorry like you drive your passenger truck. You wanna sit down and feel that dead load trying to take the steering from your hand. You kidding? There is a hundred spirits in every guy of timber trying to do you down cause you've trapped them in, see? There is a spirit in hell for every guy of timber. [*Feels around his neck and brings out a talisman on a string.*]

You reckon a guy just goes and cuts down a guy of timber. You gorra do it proper man or you won't live to cut another log. Dead men tell no tales kid. Until that guy is sawn up and turned to a bench or table, the spirit guy is still struggling inside it, and I don't fool around with him see, cause if your home was cut down you sure gonna be real crazy with the guy who's done it.

KOTONU: Yeah, I suppose so.

SAMSON: You don't believe that rubbish do you?

SAY T.: You call it rubbish! Well you tell me. Why ain't I cut and
bruised like all those guys? Cause timber don't turn against
her own son see? I'm a son of timber. And I only drive
timber see?

THUG: Son of timber!

SAY T.: That me kid. A guy is gorra have his principles. I'm a
right guy. I mean you just look arrit this way. If you gonna
be killed by a car, you don't wanna be killed by a Volks-
wagen. You wanra Limousine, a Ponriac or something
like that. Well thas my principle. Suppose you was to come
and find me in the ditch one day with one of them timber
guys on ma back. Now ain't it gonna be a disgrace if the
guy was some kinda cheap, wretched firewood full of ants
and borers. So when I carry a guy of timber, its gorra be
the biggest. One or two. If it's one, its gorra fill the whole
lorry, no room even for the wedge. And high class timber
kid. High class. Golden walnut. Obeche. Ironwood. Black
Afara. Iroko. Ebony. Camwood. And the heartwood's
gorra be sound. [*Thumps his chest.*] It's gorra have a solid
beat like that. Like mahogany.

THUG: No dirty timber!

SAY T.: Timber is ma line. You show me the wood and I'll tell
you whar kinda insects gonna attack it, and I'll tell you how
you take the skin off. And I'll tell you whar kinda spirit
is gonna be chasing you when you cut it down. If you ain't
gorra strong head kid, you can't drive no guy of timber.

SAMSON: Just the same, it doesn't much matter what you are
carrying when it rolls over you.

SAY T.: You kidding? Just you speak for yourself man. And when
that guy of timber gits real angry and plays me rough, I
just don't wan no passenger piss running on ma head. You
know, just last week I pass an accident on the road. There
was a dead dame and you know what her pretty head was

smeared with? Yam porrage. See whar I mean? A swell dame is gonna die on the road just so the next passenger kin smear her head in yam porrage? No sirree. I ain't going with no one unless with ma own guy of timber.

[*The drummer beats louder and raises a heavy, drowsy voice.*]

Eni r'oro ke juba

Ohun oju ri

K'o ba de'le a mo'ra

Ohun oju ri

Eni r'oro ke juba

Ohun oju ri

Ko ba de'le a ru'bo

Ohun oju ri

B'e de dele d'ojumo

Ohun oju ri

Oruwo re a pitan

Ohun oju ri

Eni r'esu ke yago

Ohun oju ri

Eni s'agbere f'elegun

Ohun oju ri

[*The slow song and drugged movements pick up tempo, interpolated with war-whoops and yells until the sound of the truck is heard and they stamp out to a violent beat and somersaulting war-dance, hoisting up Particulars Joe and bearing him out.*]

SAMSON [*shouting after them.*]: I hope you all get beaten up!

[*Almost immediately, from the church side of the shack comes violent knocking.*]

Now what other lunatics are those?

[*Three men are outside, within the shadow cast by the shack. Two are drivers, the third is obviously a car owner, well dressed in a rich agbada. They take turns to speak.*]

1ST MAN: Open up. Come on now, open up the shop. We've waited just about enough. It's a whole week since Sergeant Burma died, what are you waiting for?

2ND MAN: Is business to stand still while you laze around sleeping and drinking tombo? Even old wrecks go on wheels, let's see the tyres.

3RD MAN: I could use a hub with mine. Come on open up the shop.

1ST MAN: And I want that cap all drivers favour. A six-inch visor in tinted plastic. Goes over the eye and cheats the sun.

2ND MAN: He must have plenty. Where is the man? Kotonu! Don't you know the morning is half the day?

1ST MAN: Professor chose you, we're not complaining. But man you've got to give us service.

2ND MAN: Kotonu! [*Bangs again on the wall.*] Makes a man wish Sergeant Burma were alive.

3RD MAN: He would never waste a day. If he wasn't there his wife deputised.

1ST MAN: If she wasn't there you helped yourself. Accounts to be settled on the twenty-punctual.

2ND MAN: Month-ending na debt-ending. Sergeant Burma never hear excuse.

3RD MAN: If you no settle here you go settle am for heaven.

ALL: No he never let us down. Sergeant Burma never let us down.

SAMSON: Shoo shoo, you no dey sleep for house?

1ST MAN: Abi dis one craze. Wis kin sleep for this time?

2ND MAN: Tell am make 'e come open shop.

3RD MAN: You tink say weself we no sabbe sleep?

SAMSON: 'E no well. No worry am.

1ST MAN: 'E no well 'e no well, na dat one we go chop? Call am make e comot onetime.

2ND MAN: This Kotonu na failure. Wetin 'e think 'e be?

3RD MAN: Where is Professor? We will have to tell the old man.

1ST MAN: But he doesn't come till evening when the church shadow is on the shack.

2ND MAN: Well he's somewhere on the road, let's go try and dig him out.

3RD MAN: Oh but this is nonsense. Burma never let us down.

ALL: No he never let us down.

1ST MAN: Spare plugs, fuses, petrol cover.

2ND MAN: Windscreen wiper twin carburettor.

3RD MAN: Tyre chassis hub or tie-rod.

1ST MAN: Propeller pistons rings or battery

2ND MAN: Rugs car radio brakes silencer

ALL: Where there is crish-crash call Sergeant Burma

1ST MAN: Every seam of second-hand clothing

2ND MAN: Trousers sandals ties assorted

3RD MAN: Handbags lipstick cigarette holder

1ST MAN: Toys for children, springs and crankshaft

2ND MAN: Hoods umbrellas, poor Sergeant Burma

ALL: No he never let us down, no he never quit his post.

1ST MAN: Let's go. We'll get Professor to chase this one.

2ND MAN: Call himself a petty-trader?

3RD MAN: He's giving a bad name to Bosikona.

1ST MAN: Him! Trying to step in Burma's boots.

2ND MAN: If Burma's a soldier, he's a boy scout.

3RD MAN: His days are numbered. Let's get Professor. [*Going.*]

1ST MAN: Oh Sergeant Burma how we miss you.

ALL: No he never let us down. Burma never let us down. [*Off-stage by now.*]

[*Enter Salubi, dog-tired. He carries a bowl of soup and a mound of eba wrapped in leaves.*]

SALUBI: No luck. And my legs are dead.

SAMSON: You should leave them in your trousers and starch them with your clothes.

SALUBI: It is no joking matter.

SAMSON: I wish you would take a bath. I could smell your
approach five minutes before you came in.

SALUBI: Good for you. And I hope you get your Kotonu back
on the road soon so I can have some peace.

SAMSON: And I hope you get your Yessah Yessah job soon so
we can breathe some fresh air.

SALUBI: You are just like a haggling market woman. Why
don't you go and get your fresh air from the motor park.
Before you two came I used to have a clear three hours
here by myself, three hours of peace before the others start
to drift here and bite their finger-nails.

SAMSON: And pick lice off their bodies—don't leave out your
own speciality.

[*Salubi opens his mouth to reply, gives up and sits down to his
meal. He has just stirred the soup with his finger when Samson
pounces on him.*]

SAMSON: What is that? You haven't got stockfish in there have
you?

SALUBI: Stockfish? Oh you mean this panla? Certainly!

SAMSON: The whole world is surely determined to ruin me. Get
it out of here quickly.

SALUBI: What are you talking about? Do you know any self-
respecting driver who will eat eba without panla?

SAMSON [*clamps his hand over Salubi's mouth and throws an
apprehensive glance at Kotonu.*]: Shut up for heaven's sake!
Don't I have enough trouble without you coming to add
to it with your rubbishy tastes?

SALUBI: Eh, wait a minute.

SAMSON [*helping him to remove the foodstuffs.*]: Just get it out of
here.

SALUBI: What is all this? You haven't any right to drive me out
of here. Professor doesn't mind me at all.

SAMSON: That is what you think. But he particularly objects to

stockfish. He says the smell disturbs his spirits. Now go out
before he comes and catches you here.

SALUBI: I don't believe that lie.

SAMSON: You are lucky Kotonu is asleep. The Professor put him
in charge against that sort of thing. If he wakes up he will
report you and the Professor will deal with you.

SALUBI [*scampering.*]: Don't think you can frighten me with that.
I don't care one panla for your Professor. He can't do me
anything.

SAMSON: Good. Very good. I'll tell him when he comes. I'll tell
him about this morning. And he'll send the word to get
you in the dead of night.

SALUBI: Tell him if you like. One of these days the police will
catch up with him. And they'll put him where he belongs—
in the lunatic asylum of the prison. Don't think you can
scare me with that word business.

SAMSON: Just go out. I will deliver your message. [*Ushering him
out.*]

SALUBI: Deliver it. I don't care. Or do you think I don't know
about the church funds? Tell him the day the police catch
him I will come and testify against him. The man is a
menace. Pulling up road-signs and talking all that mumbo-
jumbo.

SAMSON: Yes, yes, I'll tell him. But don't ever bring stockfish
in here again.

SALUBI: A bit of stockfish won't do his brain any harm—you
tell him that.

[*Samson drives him out. Looks anxiously towards Kotonu and
appears satisfied that he hasn't overheard. Begins to pace up and
down. Stops, tip-toes past Kotonu and tries to see into the stall
through a gap in the wood.*]

KOTONU: I didn't lock it. Just remove the board.

[*Samson jumps, walks away angrily.*]

SAMSON: Who do you think is interested in your morbid
　　merchandise?

KOTONU: I never said you were.

SAMSON: Just the same, you astonish me. There are many sides
　　to you which I have never suspected. I mean, to think that
　　we grew up together.

KOTONU: I wish you would stop walking up and down. I am
　　trying to sleep.

SAMSON: Shouldn't you open up shop. Somebody might want
　　a dripping cushion from the last crash.

KOTONU: I haven't begun selling yet. Need a few more days to
　　work myself up to it.

SAMSON: Who do you think you are fooling? Didn't you sell
　　Salubi his uniform?

KOTONU: I didn't sell him anything. He stole it. I saw him take
　　it so I said he was welcome to keep it.

SAMSON: He didn't buy it?

KOTONU: I gave it to him.

SAMSON: That man not only stinks like Lagos lagoon, he lies
　　like a Lagos girl.

KOTONU: Leave him alone. Why do you keep on at him?

SAMSON: I'll tell you why. He is waiting to take your licence.

KOTONU: Well why doesn't he say so?

SAMSON: Oh he won't say a thing you can count on that.
　　But he keeps hanging around so he can buy it cheap
　　off you. Then Professor will perform his artistry
　　on it.

KOTONU: When he comes tell him he can have it.

SAMSON: I'd sooner give it to a dog. In fact give it to me now.
　　I no longer trust you with it.

KOTONU: Take it. It is hanging up over there.

　　[*Samson retrieves the licence, puts it in his pocket.*]

SAMSON: At least I will see that we get a decent price for it—and

not from any smelly monkey in uniform either. Nine years
we have been together and now all you want to do is be a
shop-keeper.

KOTONU: And sleep.

SAMSON: Yes sleep. Stay in one spot like a spider. And what
about me? How am I to live without the running-board of
a passenger lorry?

KOTONU: There are so many drivers looking for a good
conductor. One of them will take you.

SAMSON: Yes. One of them will take me. Nine years we have
worked together, and now you want me to go and join any
driver who happens along.

KOTONU: Suppose I had got killed in an accident? It could have
been us at the bridge.

SAMSON: But it wasn't. The other lorry overtook us—that's
divine providence for you.

KOTONU: One mile. Only one more mile and we would have
been first at the bridge.

SAMSON [*angry.*]: Why do you keep on about it? They overtook
us—that's their luck. It was anybody's chance.
[*He walks about the room. Stops to look at the spider.*]

SAMSON: Your brother is having a dinner. Hm. Just the wings
left of that fly.

KOTONU: The road and the spider lie gloating, then the fly
buzzes along like a happy fool . . .

SAMSON [*very hurriedly.*]: All right all right.

KOTONU: But why they and not us? Their names weren't
carved on the rotten wood.

SAMSON [*walking rapidly away from the corner.*]: All right I've
heard you. I can understand. I am not deaf.

KOTONU: What's the matter? I was only trying to understand.

SAMSON: I don't want to know. Just don't give up driving
that's all I am trying to tell you. [*Kotonu shrugs, relapses.*] I

mean, just look at it like a reasonable man. What else are
you good for? Nothing.

[*Professor enters from the side of the church. With dignified
caution he looks round to make sure he is not observed. Looks
through the open window as if he is peeping through a narrow
chink. Tests the walls with his walking stick. Pokes crevices in
the wall for signs of weakening. Shakes his head sadly, crosses
the road to the shack.*]

SAMSON: Such a sinful waste of talent. There isn't any driver in
the whole of Africa who commands the steering wheel like
you.

KOTONU: Oh let a man sleep can't you?

[*Samson sees Professor, rushes to relieve him of his bundles and
sets them on the table. Professor gives him a very condescending
nod, lays aside his stick very carefully.*

*Methodically he stacks the bundles on one side of the table,
removes pen, pencil, rubber and some paper from his pockets and
sets them out before him. Samson watches this daily ritual in rapt
fascination.*

*From his waistcoat the Professor now pulls out a pocket-watch
by the chain, examines the time and winds it.*]

SAMSON: How is the Word today Professor?

PROF.: Trapped. Fast in demonic bondage. I looked at the walls.
They have not begun to give. But I can wait. Continue the
search with patience. Avoid mirages—had one this
morning. If it had happened on a hot afternoon with the
sun heavy on the tar, I could understand. That's the hour of
mirages. But a mirage in the morning! No matter. I am
prepared now—they shan't fool me again.

[*He extracts a newspaper from a bundle and begins to study it,
using a hand lens. Samson tip-toes back to Kotonu.*]

SAMSON: Why don't we ask him what he thinks about it?

[*Kotonu pretends to have fallen asleep.*]

Answer. I know you're not asleep.

KOTONU: Yes, yes, ask him anything.

SAMSON[*goes over, timidly.*]: Please sir ... sir ... Professor ... sir ... [*Professor looks up.*] I ... we ... my friend and I, we wonder if you would favour us with your opinion on a very delicate matter.

PROF.: You are consulting me?

SAMSON: Yes Sir, we would value your opinion very much.

PROF. [*with emphasis.*]: This is a consultation.

SAMSON: Oh I am sorry, very sorry sir. I was a little forgetful. [*He fishes out a threepence and places it on the table. But Professor continues to look straight ahead of him. Nervously Samson adds a penny. Then another. He is about to add a third but he decides to protest.*] But Professor, we are both out of a job.

PROF. [*looks at him, then at the money. Shrugs, puts the coins in his pocket.*]: All right then, but only for you. If you let anyone know I will give you the full bill. My kindness would be plagued by beggars if I gave them a chance.

SAMSON[*gratefully.*]: Oh I won't breathe a word I swear. You really are a kind person.

PROF. [*affixes his monocle and stares hard at Samson.*]: Hm. I would say your problem is straightforward. You are in some kind of difficulty.

SAMSON: You have stated it exactly sir.

PROF.: In fact, one might almost say that you are about to pass through a crisis of decisions.

SAMSON: Ah, I don't know that one Professor.

PROF.: How could you? You are illiterate. It is lucky for you that I watch over you, over all of you.

SAMSON: Yes sir. Er, about our problem sir ...

PROF.: Life is difficult for the faithless. But do not despair.

SAMSON: Yes Professor. Now about our difficulty sir. As you know sir, my friend used to be a driver.

PROF.: He has a new job—with a millionaire.

SAMSON: Who? Oh he ... er ... he resigned ... no he was sacked. He told me himself, he says he was sacked when he accompanied you somewhere.

PROF.: You accuse me perhaps of ... sabotage?

SAMSON: Me sir? Not in the least, the thought never crossed my mind. Please Professor just forget that whole business, forget it altogether. It is just that he never wanted to drive anyway, and that's his trouble.

PROF.: Increase his salary.

SAMSON: No sir, it isn't that. He simply doesn't want to drive at all. I mean Professor, I have been his apprentice for the past nine years. And now he wants to give up. He doesn't want to touch another steering wheel—except as spare part of course.

PROF.: He'll lose his pension.

SAMSON: There is no pension in the job.

PROF.: What! No pension? What is your Trade Union doing about it?

SAMSON: Professor, what I mean is, how can a man cut off part of himself like that. Just look at him. He is not complete without a motor lorry.

PROF.: He is not? [*Turns to stare at Kotonu.*] What sort of an animal is he?

SAMSON: Animal? I mean to say, Professor! Ask anybody here. Everybody knows Kotonu. From Lagos to Monrovia they know him. And they know Samson his mate, his apprentice, his conductor and passenger collector. Look Professor, the road won't be the same without him.

PROF.: He was a road mender too?

SAMSON: Sir? But I told you he is a driver.

PROF. [*takes out his watch and looks at it.*]: Hm.

SAMSON: Is it working now Professor?

PROF.: No. But it still tells the time.

KOTONU [*sitting up.*]: Isn't Murano here?

SAMSON [*agitatedly.*]: You see Professor. Now Murano has become his evensong.

PROF. [*looks up at the church window.*]: It is not yet the hour of sacrament.

SAMSON [*turns angrily to Kotonu.*]: That is all you want to do now. Sit here dropping saliva until Murano turns up.

KOTONU: What's wrong with that. I say I want to retire.

SAMSON: People retire at sixty—like Professor here.

PROF. [*without looking up.*]: A small correction—I am not yet sixty. Fifty-nine pounds seven shillings and twenty-one pence—that is my real age.

KOTONU: And build up the business.

SAMSON: Yes. By giving away uniforms to anyone who can steal one. You fancy yourself a business man don't you?

KOTONU: Why not? Sergeant Burma didn't do badly. If he could do it so can I.

SAMSON: Look Professor, help me to talk to him. It is just what our people say—the man with a head is looking for a cap and the man with a cap lacks the head. When you think how much a licence costs in this place.

KOTONU: I'm not complaining.

SAMSON: Why should you? I paid for your licence. But I don't complain because it was a good investment. Was.

KOTONU: Yes, was. Until this. [*From the store he pulls out a full Ogun mask, held in shape with sticks.*]

SAMSON: I don't know why you still retain that!

KOTONU: It has to stay with me. [*Bows deeply.*]
My humble quota to the harvest of the road.
[*Drops it suddenly.*] God, God, if only I had never taken your money for my driving test.

SAMSON: It would only have grown mould where I buried it.

You see Professor, the magic of a motor engine
simply refused to reveal itself to me. Kotonu was the
clever one. From the word go he could drive better
than Indian Charlie. Oh, Indian Charlie was our master.
God rest his soul in peace but that man nearly murdered
me. Fai fai fai! Every day forty slaps at least. So I knew
that driving was not meant for people like me. I gave my
savings to Kotonu for his test.

KOTONU: I should never have taken it.

SAMSON: It would only have rotted underground. I couldn't
use it for anything else but my licence fee. That's why I
buried it in the churchyard.

PROF.: You buried it where?

SAMSON: In the churchyard. I put it in a cigarette tin and buried
it near a gravestone. And I swore there and then that if I
uprooted it for any other purpose all the spirits in that
burial-ground should follow me home and haunt me for
three days and nights.

PROF.: Very risky. Very risky. Conjuration is no light matter
you know. Never fool around with spirits.

SAMSON: Oh I know that. But it came to the same thing really
because I used it for Kotonu and he took me on as his
partner.

PROF.: You know the Word?

SAMSON: What is that Professor?

PROF.: Oh the conceit of insects! The butterfly thinks the flapping
of his wings fathered the whirlwind that followed. The
burrowing beetle feels he powered the arm of the eruption.
Do you claim to have communed with spirits in the last
repository of damned souls?

SAMSON: I only said I kept my money there.

PROF.: So the dead are now your bank managers?

SAMSON: No sir, I . . .

PROF.: No harm in it, no harm in it. Do they give overdrafts
though?

SAMSON: Well I only kept the money in a cigarette tin.

PROF.: But you couldn't have known the Word could you? A
gravestone turns slow and gentle on the hinge; angels
trapped by day in illusions of concrete rise in night's
parole; the dead earth opens at your feet—my friend,
confronted with the Resurrection, would you know the
Word?

SAMSON: Would I what what Professor?

PROF.: Daylight marble lies! Oh mocking God! To think that
even worms were given the Word—else why do they hold
our flesh in such contempt?

SAMSON: Do you mean for instance, if Kotonu died now and I
met him at night?

PROF.: Would you know the Word?

SAMSON: Well I don't know which word. But I might try Our
Father which art in Heaven and take to my heels.

PROF.: And your friend. Does he know the Word?

SAMSON: Kotonu.

KOTONU: Hm.

SAMSON: The Professor is talking to you. He says what would
you say in the cemetery.

PROF.: You reduce it all to nonsense burying your faith in
cigarette tins. You should invest it. My friend, the Word is
a living word not a grave-robber's prayer of appeasement.

SAMSON [*highly indignant.*]: I am not a grave-robber. I tell you it
was my own money. I kept it there in a cigarette tin. It was
there for two years before I even touched it.
[*He walks over distractedly to the corner, looks at the web.*]
Oh, he's finished.

KOTONU: He is never finished, he's only resting.

SAMSON: I don't mean the Professor. Your dining brother.

KOTONU: I wonder which driver that was. Or maybe a passenger.

SAMSON [*furiously.*]: Oh yes just go on. Now I have started you off you won't let us rest. Why don't you just admit you are tired?

KOTONU: But I've said so already.

[*Salubi rushes in. Stops, then goes straight for the Professor.*]

SALUBI: Professor, I need a licence.

PROF.: It is past my hour of consultation.

SALUBI: Oh, an oversight. Forgive me sir. [*Places a shilling on the desk.*]

PROF. [*picks up the shilling and affixes his monocle.*]: At a glance, I would say that you need some sort of official document.

SALUBI: Oh yes sir. A driving licence. Such a chance professor— I knew it would come if I persevered.

PROF.: I would also deduce that your need is somewhat urgent.

SALUBI: Desperate sir. I must get a licence now now. This job is first class. If I don't get it I will commit suicide.

PROF.: God rot your coward bones! Do you think not enough people die here that you must come and threaten me with death? You spurious spew. You instrument of mortgage. You unlicensed appendage of the steering wheel—[*throws the shilling out of door.*] I refuse to touch your case.

SALUBI [*prostrating flat on his belly.*]: Oga I beg you sir. I sorry too much. I will never do so again sir.

PROF. [*in mounting rage.*]: Get out. Get out! And don't let me see you in here again. Do you think I keep pews at the waking for any false contractor to death. Suicide! May the elusive Word crack your bones in a hundred splinters!

SALUBI [*cowers, terror-stricken.*]: Professor I beg you, not that. Anything but that.

PROF.: May your tongue of deception be rotted in pestilence from the enigma of the Inviolate Word.

SAMSON: Professor sir, Professor . . .

SALUBI: Professor, I beg you in the name of your father, no put that your conjuration on top me head. Kotonu . . . help me beg him . . .

SAMSON: Sir, please sir, he won't do so again. I will vouch for him—he won't do so again.

PROF.: Get out of my sight, and the Word follow you as you leave my threshold.

[*He sits, plunges himself straight into his usual occupation with the papers.*]

SALUBI: Kotonu, won't you people put in a word for me? I swear I won't do so again. Never say die sir. Never say die —that is my motto from now on. I will paint it on every lorry I see—Never say die! Samson, help me now. Tell Professor to take in curse commot for my head. Enh. Samson call me I beg you, call me make Professor hear me answer to my motto.

SAMSON: Salubi.

SALUBI: Never say die!

SAMSON: Salubi Salubirity.

SALUBI: Never say die.

SAMSON: Salubi omo agbepo.

SALUBI [*hesitates a fraction but Samson is unyielding.*]: Never say die.

SAMSON: You mout' stink like night-soil lorry.

SALUBI: Never say die.

SAMSON: Your body and lice day like David and Jonathan.

SALUBI: Never say die.

SAMSON: Ole ngboro fear no foe rob in own grandmamma.

SALUBI: Never say die.

SAMSON: Iwin ogodo. Ten like you and soap-factories close down.

SALUBI: Never say die.

SAMSON: Professor sir, I think he is truly repentant. Kotonu and I, we beg you to forgive him.

[*Receiving no response, he turns his back, takes some money from a deep pocket and returns to Professor. Half-way he stops, goes to Salubi and rifles his pocket for more money, all of which he places very apologetically on the table.*]

PROF. [*without bothering to look.*]: And double the usual consultation fee.

SALUBI [*leaps up like a man reprieved from death.*]: Yes sir, anything sir. I am so very thankful I swear I will never do so again. [*Puts the money on the table and prostrates himself.*] Ah I thank you Professor. I thank you very much. It's my ignorance sir, don't be vexing with me like that. After all a father doesn't to vex with his children like that.

PROF.: Photograph?

SALUBI [*rapidly producing two snapshots.*]: Here sir. Everything is ready.

PROF.: Are you an escaped convict? This photo looks villanous.

SALUBI: Me sir? But I have never go to prison in all my life.

PROF.: A gaol-bird. I know one when I see it. This photo confirms it.

SALUBI: Oga I swear . . .

PROF.: Come back tomorrow morning. You have all the smell of a prison yard about you.

SAMSON: I told you you should wash.

SALUBI: Please sir, Professor, don't disappoint me. Is a matter of life and death. Enh! I mean to say . . . [*He stops short, horrified at what Professor's reaction would be.*]

PROF. [*gives him a long cold stare.*]: Get him outside before I change my mind. [*The man retreats, goes over to one of the benches and tucks himself unobtrusively in a corner.*]

PROF.: Outside. Outside. [*Salubi runs out.*]

SAMSON [*follows him and looks out. Salubi is crouching near the door.*]: I thought so. Dead scared like that but he can't even go away. And why?

KOTONU [*sitting up.*]: Why? But you heard the man, he wants his licence.

SAMSON: He knows Professor will take his own time. No it's because Murano will soon arrive. That is how you will become if you give up driving. You are lucky Murano doesn't know how you all depend on him.

KOTONU: He is late today.

PROF. [*looks at the church window.*]: He'll come at the communion hour. When that shadow covers me in grace of darkness he will come.

KOTONU: Yes, he always seems to time it well.

PROF.: They cannot cast me out. I will live in the shadow of the fort. I will question the very walls for the hidden Word.

KOTONU: If I may ask, Professor, where did you find Murano?

PROF.: Neglected in the back of a hearse. And dying. Moaned like a dog whose legs have been broken by a motor car. I took him—somewhere—looked after him till he was well again.

KOTONU: And you set him to tap palm wine for you?

PROF. [*rises, goes over to Kotonu.*]: I think you are an astute man, or simply desperate. You grope towards Murano, the one person in this world in whom the Word reposes.

SAMSON: Much use that is to him. He cannot use his tongue.

PROF.: Deep. Silent but deep. Oh my friend, beware the pity of those that have no tongue for they have been proclaimed sole guardians of the Word. They have slept beyond the portals of secrets. They have pierced the guard of eternity and unearthed the Word, a golden nugget on the tongue. And so their tongue hangs heavy and they are forever silenced. Do you mean you do not see that Murano has one leg longer than the other?

SAMSON: Murano? But his legs are the same.

PROF.: Blind!

KOTONU: Oh I admit he limps. Anyway he seems okay to me.

PROF.: When a man has one leg in each world, his legs are never the same. The big toe of Murano's foot—the left one of course—rests on the slumbering chrysalis of the Word. When that crust cracks my friends—you and I, that is the moment we await. That is the moment of our rehabilitation. When that crust cracks . . . [*Growing rapidly emotional, he stops suddenly, sniffs once or twice, wipes his misted glasses, returns briskly to his table.*]

SAMSON [*goes over to Kotonu.*]: I have often thought of following that Murano you know. He sets out about five o'clock in the morning, goes in that direction. And he doesn't come back until five in the afternoon. That's a long time to tap a little wine. Have you ever considered where he goes?

KOTONU: Why should I?

SAMSON: One of these days I will follow him some of the way . . .

PROF. [*sharply.*]: You are tired of life perhaps?

SAMSON: I didn't say anything.

PROF.: Those who are not equipped for strange sights—fools like you—go mad or blind when their curiousity is pursued. First find the Word. It is not enough to follow Murano at dawn and spy on him like a vulgar housewife. Find the Word.

SAMSON [*disinterested.*]: Where does one find it Professor?

PROF.: Where? Where ascent is broken and a winged secret plummets back to earth. Ask Murano.

SAMSON: But he cannot talk.

PROF. [*cunningly.*]: You see. They know what they are doing. [*Enter two of the lay-abouts, with broken heads. One collapses on a bench and the other rushes through to the water-pot, drinks like a camel, pours the rest over his head and slides down beside the pot. Professor looks at them with anger then returns to his work with a ferocious concentration.*]

SAMSON [*timidly.*]: Professor, if you could just find one word to persuade Kotonu not to give up driving, I would be satisfied with that.

PROF. [*hits the table suddenly.*]: That's it! I knew there was something I had forgotten. A solution, a compensation, a redress, a balance of inequalities... bring me your friend's driving licence.

SAMSON [*reaching for it.*]: You think it might be in the licence Professor?

PROF.: What?

SAMSON: The Word.

PROF.: Do you think I spend every living moment looking for that? What do you think I am—a madman? [*Puts on a pair of glasses and examines the licence carefully with the additional aid of the hand lens. Places Salubi's photograph over Kotonu's. Sighs. Sadly.*] It is a sign of my failing powers when I am glad for alterations this easy to hand. Not so long ago I would have spurned such clumsy craftsmanship, built a new document from old electric bills and those government circulars in which food-sellers wrap their food.

[*He turns his pen on the documents.*]

SAMSON [*alarmed.*]: What are you thinking of doing Professor?

PROF.: Nearly a year since I celebrated my hundredth forgery. It is difficult always to forge from scratch, and I am getting old. Once I could do three licences in a week and not feel the strain. Now if I manage one, I feel the life has gone from me. This needs only a little adjustment. A neat transfer, not a basic forgery.

SAMSON: But Professor, what about us? Our livelihood! I asked you to convince him to return to the road but you want to cut him out altogether. What will we live on?

PROF.: He will find the Word.

SAMSON: The Word? Will that fill his belly or mine?

PROF.: Samson. Lion-hearted Samson with an ass's head, can you not see that your friend will never drive again?

SAMSON: How do you know? It is only a phase and he will get over it.

PROF. [*pierces him with a sudden prolonged earnestness*.]: Tell me my friend, were you ever a millionaire?

SAMSON: What . . . who er me . . . I don't understand professor.

PROF.: I had a strange experience this morning. Missed my way and was received into the palace of millionaire. Your friend guided me out or I might still be lost and wandering. In return I took him to the latest offering of the Word. I have accepted him—and you—like the others. Where do you come from? When do you take leave of me? [*He shrugs.*] But there, as the blood and the waste clung to his feet, I knew him. And I tell you, before my eyes, he was touched.

SAMSON: I could have told you that. He is self-indulgent with feeling.

PROF.: No no, not that. He was touched [*Looks round at Kotonu and then taps his head.*]—here. I've known madmen on both sides of the grave, but he . . . [*Shakes his head, pitying.*] Don't expect him to drive again.

SAMSON: He will. He must. He knows no other life but driving, he can use his hands for no other purpose than to turn the heavy wheel, and to throw that wretched gear which I never mastered.

PROF.: And you I suppose think you cannot breathe unless you are swinging on the tailboard and the exhaust pipe is puffing poison in your face?

SAMSON [*amazed.*]: You understand it Professor sir. I mean, for a man of books, you really do. But please help him understand it. We were pupils together, and I know he was conceived in the back of a lorry.

KOTONU: Samson! I was only born in a lorry.

SAMSON: Oh what do you know? Believe me Professor, his father used to tell me some things which would shock you sir. Even if you are a man of the world it would still shock you. He used to talk to me as if I was a grown man.

PROF.: He had a father?

SAMSON: Oh yes. He was a truck-pusher, they called him Kokol'ori. He was the first of the truck-pushers and the randiest between Obalende and Agege. You know Professor, those who came after him ended up with big transport business, but not his father. He began with one truck and he ended up with that same truck. The only change was that he covered the wooden wheels with rubber.

PROF.: Ah, another man ruined by kindness!

SAMSON: Kind? Kotonu's father kind? He was too fond of women that's all. A truck-pusher now, who are his greatest customers?

PROF. [*indignantly*.]: I have never dabbled in that trade.

SAMSON: Women traders sir. The market women. They are the backbone of Omolanke transport business. But Kokol'ori would not take a penny from them. Instead, he made honeymoon with them. Anywhere. In the back of the stalls, under Carter Bridge . . . in the truck itself. Once he was locked up in a cell. Where others would have broken out and escaped, he broke into an adjoining cell where a woman was detained and spent the night with her. Oh he used to tell me all his adventures. In fact I used to be the go-between for all his doings. He was sensitive that way, he would never use his own son, so Kotonu doesn't really know much about his affairs.

[*Enter three more of the touts, supporting one another. They flop down like a defeated army.*]

PROF. [*staring at the gang with truly terrifying venom.*]: Mortify his flesh. Sentence him to mortify his flesh.

KOTONU: Oh it's too late now. He's dead.

SAMSON: Kotonu and I grew up together helping him to push the truck. [*Confidentially to the Professor.*] You know Kotonu was really conceived in a push-truck. Kolol'ori told me himself. He said he parked the truck on a slight rise in the ground and when he began to make honeymoon on top of Kotonu's mother, the truck started to roll downhill. Perhaps that was why he was so fond of him. Of all his sons Kotonu was the only one he would acknowledge. [*Professor, increasingly scandalized, looks relieved at last.*]

PROF.: Well, at least he was legitimate.

SAMSON: Oh yes. The push-truck had a licence. And a genuine licence too, not like one of yours.

KOTONU: He left me the truck.

SAMSON: He had little else to leave. Just the truck.

KOTONU: He died before I became a driver. If he had been alive he would have slept with six women, to celebrate my becoming a driver. But he died before that, of a lorry in his back. It beat his spine against a load of stockfish. It was what he carried mostly—stockfish. That day the truck was piled high with it. [*The group begins to dirge softly.*]

SAMSON: We were both there. Pulling the truck in front while he pushed behind. The bales of stockfish nearly reached the sky. If Carter Bridge had been joined above the road, the load of dried fish would have touched it. We were thrown forward . . .

KOTONU: Buried in stockfish. It was all I remembered for a long

time, the smell of stockfish. Torn bodies on the road all
smell of stockfish have you noticed?
[*The dirge wells up gradually.*]

SAMSON [*whispering.*]: Professor, Professor ...

PROF. [*turns hurriedly to studying his papers.*]: I'm busy.

SAMSON: But what are you going to do about it sir? If he doesn't
drive the boss will take the lorry from us.

PROF.: Let me concentrate will you! Take your lives away from
me or I will drive you out.
[*The dirge continues.*]

>   Iri se l'oganjo orun ni ki lo ti je
>   Iri se l'oganjo orun ni ki lo s'orun
>   Iri erun ta si mi l'ese iku gb'omi tan
>   Iri erun ta si mi l'aiya otutu eru mu mi
>   Iku se ni o, akoni l'aiye lo
>   E ba mi kedun, Kokolori o ...

SAMSON: But Professor sir ...

PROF. [*shouting above the dirge.*]: Leave me. Leave me. You
intrude your persons on me. I offer you shelter, nothing
more. Leave me or lose yourself in obscurity like all who
come here. Who gave you leave to demand this preference?
Get out of my sight.

SAMSON [*almost tearfully.*]: But you must help me. He is going to
become like the others. In a month he will lose the touch
and he will have to drift back here for a pick-me-up.

PROF.: Oh you think you are special enh? Different from the rest
of them. You think there is something degrading in taking
shelter under my wings? [*Turns on the singers with sudden
fierceness.*] And stop that disgusting wail you rejects of the
road.
[*The singing stops at once. they cower before his rage which
mounts as he speaks.*]
Vermin. Judases you god-forsaken judases you sell your

bodies and you have just done again have you not? You think you are reckless and brave but how can a stupid ox or a runaway train talk of courage. I offer you a purpose but you take unmeaning risks which means I, I must wait and hope that you return alive to fulfil the course I have drawn for you, so you sell again and again for the lure of money.

THUG: But Professor we need the loot.

PROF.: Shut up! Shut your mercenary mouth!

[*The thug gives up. Abruptly Professor takes up his work.*]

SAMSON [*with much hesitation.*]: You shouldn't waste your time on those boma boys Professor . . .

PROF. [*putting down his work, stares him calmly in the eye.*]: What do *you* want? [*Samson fidgets, losing courage.*] Well?

SAMSON: It's nothing Professor, nothing.

PROF.: What sound is that?

[*An increasing rumble of metallic wheels on stones. The lay-abouts, recognizing the meaning, become newly sobered, take off their caps in respect. Kotonu has leapt up, staring in the direction of the noise.*]

PROF. [*more insistently.*]: What is that sound?

SAMSON: They are bringing them in Professor. The accident on the bridge.

PROF.: And must they so noise their presence about? Waste! Waste! I never knew them. How can they tell me anything?

SAMSON: They are coming in for mass burial.

[*The black side of a lorry moves slowly past, blotting out the interior of the shack with its shadow, moves towards the church in which lights are now seen through the open window. Only this light now permeates the shack.*]

PROF.: Oh I could preach them such a sermon for the occasion, I could awaken pain with such memories . . .

SAMSON: Oh yes you could Professor. We still remember the days . . .

[*The organ leading, the choir begin a funeral hymn.*]

PROF. [*shakes his head sadly.*]: The choir began off key. By the last verse the dead will be glad they are dead.

[*The thugs begin to file out towards the church.*]

You are going over to them?

THUG: Only to wait outside and pay our last respects sir.

PROF. [*hesitates, while they wait uncertainly. Then his manner changes, becoming urgent.*]: Oh yes you must. Get out. [*To Samson.*] You too, go if you wish. And your friend.

SAMSON: I've seen enough. You forget we were there. Right behind them as they went over.

PROF.: Ah yes. You were so near . . . perhaps in that is contained a promise. But I feel cheated just the same. Such a prodigal hearse, and not one of you within it.

SAMSON [*horrified.*]: What are you saying Professor?

PROF.: Not one of you . . . cheats, you godless cheats, not one of you!

SAMSON: Do you hear him Kotonu?

KOTONU [*rising.*]: Since when did you get bothered by what Professor says? Let's go.

SAMSON: Where? The funeral?

PROF.: Leave. I want some moments' quiet. Go and join the lament for the chosen.

KOTONU: Come on.

[*They leave. Professor is alone for a few moments. Enter Murano from the opposite side, very uncertainly, his tapper's 'cradle' hung over his shoulders.*]

PROF. [*without turning.*]: I thought it might happen, that is why I let them go. Hearing the sound of the organ and the singing you would wonder if the sun had played tricks on your sight. But [*turns to him*] as you can see, it is not yet dusk. This is not our evening communion, only a requiem for departed souls. I even came this morning [*he chuckles*] I must take no chances. Morning is the time for funerals, and who knows, even they may have stumbled on that wisdom. So I . . . missed my way here—to keep watch. [*His manner changes suddenly, becoming abrupt.*] But you must return quickly, before you are seen. All faces are the same in twilight or by night. The Word needs no vulgar light of day to be manifest. Go now.

[*Footsteps are heard coming towards the door. Professor gestures desperately.*]

PROF.: Hide! Hide!

[*Murano hides just on the other side of the store. Enter Salubi, remains just inside the door scanning the room.*]

SALUBI: That's strange. [*Professor raises his head.*] I swear I saw someone sneak inside. It could be a thief.

PROF.: And you think I might need the protection of another thief?

SALUBI: No sir . . . I . . . what I mean is that I saw when the others went to the funeral so I thought someone might be coming to rob the store, knowing the place to be deserted.

PROF.: It isn't—as you see.

SALUBI [*hastily withdrawing.*]: I made a mistake . . . so sorry to disturb you at all sir, very sorry indeed. . . . [*He sees part of Murano sticking out.*] Hah!

PROF.: Are you still there?

[*Salubi makes a sign to him to be silent, pulls a knife and tip-toes backwards out of the room. Professor waits, listening hard, signs to Murano to go out the same way as Salubi. Murano moves a few steps but another sound arrests his escape—Salubi arriving to trap him from behind. Murano stays on the other side of the store. Enter Salubi, knife at the ready. Murano tip-toes round the store and comes up behind Salubi. Salubi listens, then lifts the tarpaulin suddenly and sweeps the knife in a wide curve into the space. Murano throws the cradle*]

*loop over his head and twists it. The knife drops and Salubi,
his back still turned to his assailant, struggles to tear the rope
from his neck. Desperate with fear, he flails towards Professor,
moaning for help.*]

PROF. [*looking dispassionately at the scene.*]: Perhaps . . . if you
promised not to look in his face . . . [*Salubi nods frantically,
choking*] . . . so that you could not recognize him at an identi-
fication parade . . . [*again Salubi nods, more weakly.*] Now
walk towards me, and look back only if you want to die.
[*He signs to Murano to release him. Salubi staggers down to
the Professor, chafing his neck. Murano swiftly disappears.*]

PROF. [*bending down to his work.*]: And now take your carrion
from my sight.

PART TWO

[About an hour later]

PROF.: And you brought no revelation for me? You found no broken words where the bridge swallowed them?

SAMSON: How could we think of such a thing Professor?

PROF.: A man must be alert in each event. But the store then? Surely you brought new spare parts for the store?

SAMSON: Sir . . .

PROF.: You neglect my needs and you neglect the Quest. Even total strangers have begun to notice. Three men sought me out on the road. They complained of your tardiness in re-opening the shop.

SAMSON: Oh these foolish men . . .

PROF.: Understand, that shop sustains our souls and feeds our bodies. We lose customers every day.

SAMSON: It is no use Professor. You don't know what we've been through. The man is in no condition to start trading in that kind of stuff.

PROF. [*bangs the table*.]: But you bring back nothing at all. Nothing. How do you expect me to make out your statement for the police?

SAMSON: Ah but you always manage Professor.

PROF.: On nothing? You exaggerate your notion of expressiveness in your friend's face. Call him here. [*Kotonu comes forward. Professor glares angrily at him.*] It is only a degree of coarseness, that's all. [*Rummages among the papers.*] I need a statement form. Here is one . . . now you tell me, you who return empty-handed and empty-minded, what do I write? Well? What happened at the bridge? You say

the lorry overtook you—good. [*Writes.*] Lorry was
travelling at excessive speed. You see, I can make up a
police statement that would dignify the archives of any
traffic division but tell me—have I spent all these years in
dutiful search only to wind up my last moments in
meaningless statements. What did you see friend, what did
you see? Show me the smear of blood on your brain.

KOTONU: There was this lorry . . .

PROF.: Before the event friend, before the event. Were you
accessory before the fact?

KOTONU: Even before the bridge, I saw what was yet to happen.

PROF. [*puts down the pen. Softly*—.]: You swear to that?

KOTONU: It was a full load and it took some moments overtaking
us, heavy it was.

PROF. [*writing furiously.*]: It dragged alongside and after an
eternity it pulled to the front swaying from side to side,
pregnant with stillborns. Underline—with stillborns.

SAMSON: Sensible men turn from what they may not see. Don't
you agree Professor?

PROF.: Get one of those herbalists to inoculate him then. Not
those Ministry of Health people you understand? Use the
herbalists. What's the Ministry's needle after all except for
sewing the Word together or the broken flesh. But mostly
the tattered Word. Twelve lashes everyday on his bare
back and plenty of ground peppers pasted into the tracks
that's the only effective inoculation.

KOTONU: I swear it was what I saw. The lorry was filled with
people but there was not one face among them. . . .
[*The Professor continues scribbling fast.*]

SAMSON: Because they had rags on their faces. It was only a
kola nut lorry from the North and the rear half was filled
with people. The truck was top-heavy as always. And they
had cloth on their faces to keep out the dust.

KOTONU: Oh yes the dust. The wraith of dust which pursued
them.

SAMSON: There you are, you admit it—the dust. How could you
see anything for dust? Only vague shapes . . .

KOTONU: But it cleared I tell you. Before my eyes it cleared
and I saw I was mistaken. It was an open truck and it
carried nothing but stacks and stacks of beheaded fish, and
oh God the smell of stockfish! But we caught up with
them finally . . . at the broken bridge, and you shouted—

SAMSON: Look out Kotonu! [*A violent screech of brakes.*]

KOTONU: It's all right. I've seen it.

[*They walk forward, skirt an area carefully and peer down a
hole in the ground.*]

KOTONU: I didn't know that a hearse could be this size. The
gates would never open wide enough to take it, not in our
burial-ground.

SAMSON: Don't go too near the edge. The planks are rotten.

KOTONU: This is a huge hole they've made. And the side is
completely gone.

SAMSON: For God's sake be careful!

KOTONU: You are wrong. This hole was never dug for me.

SAMSON: Does this wretched bridge look choosy to you? Just
be careful that's all.

KOTONU: I tell you the hole was never dug for me. It isn't one
mile since they overtook us remember?

SAMSON: Get off the rotten edge!

KOTONU [*coming away.*]: You fret too much.

SAMSON: Mourners stay well behind the heap of loose sands.

KOTONU: And the breast-beater threatens to follow her husband
into the grave only when the strong arms of her brothers
restrain her—oh I know that cant.

SAMSON [*laughing.*]: Be comforted they plead, and she is.
Comforted. As the reverend preacher said to his

congregation, Comfort ye my people. And the half-
illiterate interpreter said, Comfort ye—this Comfort; my
people—is my people. This Comfort, is my people.

TOGETHER: Comforti yi, enia mi ni. [*They laugh, a distinct edge
of hysteria.*]

PROF.: But there is this other joke of the fisherman, slapping a
loaded net against the sandbank. [*Looks round him.*] When
the road is dry it runs into the river. But the river? When
the river is parched what choice but this? Still it is a pleasant
trickle—reddening somewhat—between barren thighs of
an ever patient rock. The rock is a woman you understand,
so is the road. They know how to lie and wait.

SAMSON [*anxiously.*]: Kotonu . . .

PROF. [*writing.*]: Below that bridge, a black rise of buttocks, two
unyielding thighs and that red trickle like a woman washing
her monthly pain in a thin river. So many lives rush in and
out between her legs, and most of it a waste.

SAMSON: The passengers are coming out.

PROF.: Belched from the bowels of some gluttonous god . . . God
they looked so messed about.

SAMSON: Kotonu, they are coming out.

KOTONU [*fiercely.*]: Rubbish! They are dead!

SAMSON: No. I mean our own passengers. [*Turns and runs back
towards the lorry frame.*] Get back will you. Go on, get in,
it's nothing. We were just testing the bridge that's all.
Don't start delaying us you hear.

KOTONU: No no let them. It's much safer they all cross on foot.
Get them across and I'll try and edge the lorry past the gap.

SAMSON: No, first let me test the planks. I'll jump on them and
see.

KOTONU: And weaken them some more? No no, we can manage.

SAMSON: You are sure there is enough room?

KOTONU: You have begun to doubt me?

SAMSON [*turns round.*]: All right all right, come down all of you.
What is all that rubbish? No waste of time you hear? Lef'
your load, I say lef' your dirty bundle. Lef am. All right I
sorry I mo know say na your picken. Make you all walka
this side. If una wan look make you go look for other side.
You foolish people, wetin you stop dey look now? Black
man too useless, unless una get rubbish for look you no
dey satisfy. Hurry up, no waste of time. [*He runs forward
suddenly.*] God punish you, you wretched woman, why
you dey carry your picken look that kind thing? You tink
na cowboy cinema? Commot my friend . . . a-ah, these
people too foolish. Na de kind ting person dey show small
picken? If 'e begin dream bad dream and shout for night
you go rush go native doctor. Foolish woman! Na another
man calamity you fit take look cinema.
[*As he herds them across the bridge, the drivers begin dirging
softly.*]

KOTONU: We should have got there first.

SAMSON [*despondently.*]: Kill us a dog Kotonu, kill us a dog.
Kill us a dog before the hungry god lies in wait and makes
a substitute of me. That was a thin shave. A sensible man
would see it as a timely warning, but him? I doubt it. Not
for all the wealth of a traffic policeman. Dog's intestines
look messy to me he says—who asked him to like it? Ogun
likes it that's all that matters. It's his special meat. Just run
over the damned dog and leave it there, I don't ask you
to stop and scoop it up for your next dinner. Serve Ogun
his tit-bit so the road won't look at us one day and say Ho
ho you two boys you look juicy to me. But what's the use?
The one who won't give Ogun willingly will yield heavier
meat by Ogun's designing.
[*The lay-abouts stop dirging, remain standing awkwardly in
their usual place, looking uncertainly towards Samson.*]

SAMSON: Anything wrong?

THUG. We ... er ... you see Say Tokyo Kid is not here or he
would do it. So perhaps you would just say something.

SAMSON: Oh, all right. [*He composes himself as do the others, head
bowed.*] May we never walk when the road waits, famished.
[*Too late Professor covers up his ears, shaking his head angrily.
The others relax into their seats.*]

PROF. [*intensely.*]: It is lucky for you that you brought a god on to
my doorstep. I would have seared your blasphemous tongue
this instant with the righteous vengeance of the Word.

SAMSON [*almost in a general appeal.*]: But what have I done now?
[*Professor resumes his work, still much impassioned.*]
[*to Kotonu.*] Do you know what he was talking about?
What god on his doorstep?

KOTONU [*leaps up, agitated.*]: He said that? A god on his doorstep
—did he say that?

SAMSON: You heard him.

KOTONU: I must find out. Professor ...

PROF.: Re-open the shop.

KOTONU: But Professor.

PROF.: The shop my friend the shop! The shop must be
re-opened at once. I don't permit shuttered windows in my
household. [*Pointing to the church.*] They are the ones who
bar up their windows. I have nothing to hide. Have you?

KOTONU: But I must know Professor. What did you find on
your doorstep?

PROF.: I forbid you to foist your troubles on me. Open up the
shop!

KOTONU: I came to you for help. How much longer must I wait?

PROF.: Open the shop. Like you all I also wait but you do not
hear me complain.
[*Kotonu hestiates, goes to the store and disappears behind the
tarpaulin cover, begins to re-arrange the junk.*]

SAMSON [*pleads very sincerely.*]: Don't make him do it Professor
    sir. Give the store to someone else.

PROF.: I make no one do anything. But are you telling me
    Sergeant Burma was a better man? Your friend appears, if
    I may say so, to have the edge on Burma. Well, hasn't he?
    Or do you say he is inferior clay?

SAMSON: They are different people.

PROF.: I didn't open this house for different people. And he isn't.
    Sooner or later you prove it. Like flies you prove it. Like
    Rhamaddan you prove it. Like mosquito larvae on the day
    of the sanitary inspector you prove it. I have not worn my
    feet along the roads for nothing. Anyway you cannot
    neglect the material necessities of life. How does he intend
    to live since he won't drive?

SAMSON: We have savings.

PROF. [*his eyes light up.*]: You have savings?

SAMSON [*with sudden caution.*]: Well, a little. Not much you
    know. I have to do the saving for both of us.

PROF. [*affixes the monocle and stares him out.*]: How much have you
    saved?

SAMSON: Nothing much Professor, only . . .

PROF.: I must know the truth.

    [*Samson, squirming, eventually gives in. Turns his back on
    Professor, and from the deep recesses of his baggy trousers, brings
    out a pouch. Hurriedly he extracts a note from it and hides it,
    places the rest on the table.*]

    Any paper? Paper Paper. Where is the Government I.O.U.,
    the thing which promises to pay on demand.

SAMSON: Where would I get such a thing sir?

PROF. [*opens the bag at the mouth and peers into the contents.*]:
    What you ought to form is a syndicate.

SAMSON: I don't quite understand.

PROF.: You never do. Where is that scum? Go find him.

[*Samson goes. As he turns his back, Professor tries to extract a coin from the bag but Samson looks back just then. Professor is left with no choice but to carry out his action after a natural hesitation, explaining quite calmly.*]

For initial expenses you know.

SAMSON[*pokes his head around the corner.*]: Wake up. Professor wants you.

SALUBI[*jumps up and runs to Professor.*]: Is it ready sir?

PROF. [*hands him a coin.*]: Go and buy my usual. Only the puffed kind you understand. And groundnuts. Crisp ones, not soggy. Hurry up!

SALUBI: Will it be all right about the licence sir?

PROF.: Get going!

[*Salubi runs out.*]

SAMSON: With all due respects Professor sir, I don't quite see how that will come under initial expenses.

PROF.: We had to get rid of him. Or you can have him spying on us if you like.

SAMSON: But Professor, he was already outside.

PROF.: That is why it was necessary to call him in.

[*Samson scratches his head, puzzles it a bit, gives up.*]

Now what are your assets? A driving licence, and your small savings. Right? Now that creature who went out just now will pay well for his licence. I suggest half his first salary, payable in one-monthly instalments.

SAMSON: But we are not selling it.

PROF.: I'll make out the I.O.U. [*He pats the bundle of assorted papers.*] See that? Not even death can boast such a tower of I.O.Us.

SAMSON: We are not giving up the road!

PROF.: I propose we set up a syndicate, calculate the assets, decide on a policy. As a special concession I will permit you to come in as equal partners with me. I hold half the

partnership, you and your friend can have the other half.
Fifty-fifty all the way.

SAMSON: Excuse me Professor, this . . . assets as you call our
money, do you happen to have any yourself?

PROF. [*pats his paper bundles.*]: Almost too much of it. I offer you
sanctuary in my tower of words.

SAMSON [*wide-eyed.*]: You mean there is money hidden in that?
And everyone thinking you were penniless all this time!

PROF.: Money? What money?

SAMSON [*trying to peep into one end of a bundle.*]: You might even
be a millionaire and we never knew it. I always thought
you weren't as mad as people thought.

PROF. [*whips out his stick, threatening.*]: Take your snail slime
secreted eyes off the living testament before I poke them
off. Do you think I would foul up eternal beads of cowries
with minted commerce? How dare you! It is true I have
not found the Word but tempt me and I shall unleash its
elemental truths on your head.

SAMSON [*recoils, but bravely.*]: Well you always mislead a man. I
thought your assets were in there.

PROF.: And so they are you fool. Somewhere in that granary is
that elusive kernel, the Word, the Key, the moment of my
rehabilitation. From what cesspit was this object dragged
that you set it against the select harvest of a faithful gleaner?
Get it off!

[*Sweeps the pouch off the table with the stick, the coins roll out,
scattering all over the floor.*]

SAMSON [*chasing and gathering them.*]: You are a very confusing
person Professor. I can't follow you at all. Of course if
you mean I.O.Us. it makes some sense especially
government I.O.Us. Only, will they stand up in a court
of law? The ink has faded on most of them. I mean,
look at it yourself.

PROF.: When I form a syndicate, I come in on my own terms.
[*Samson hesitates and approaches the table.*]

SAMSON: But if I may make a humble suggestion sir, Professor
is not a cockroach is he?

PROF.: What are you talking about?

SAMSON: I mean, is Professor a cockroach? Or a termite?
Because, otherwise, how will that kind of asset fill his belly?
[*Professor goes back to studying the papers, underlining a phrase,
ringing a word here and there. Samson shakes his head and
proceeds to search for the remaining money.*]

KOTONU [*picks up a coin which has rolled to his feet.*]: There is one
here Samson.

SAMSON [*runs to take it.*]: Ah thank you, thank you.
[*Kotonu returns to the stall.*]
Wait. Let me take off your shoes.

KOTONU: What for?

SAMSON: A driver must have sensitive soles on his feet. Unlike
his buttocks. His buttocks would be hard. Heavy-duty
tyres. But not the feet you see. Because he does not walk so
much, and he has to be able to judge the pressure on the
pedals exactly right. I have such thick soles you see so I
always revved the engine too much or too little. Then it
was Fai! Fai! Fai! You think say I get petrol for waste?
Take your foot commot for ancelerator! Small small! I
say small small—you tink say dis one na football game. Fai
fai fai! You dey press brake—Gi-am!—as if na stud you
wan' give centre back. I say do am soft soft! Fai fai fai! All a
waste of time. Every time I started the lorry it went like a
railway—gbaga gbaga—like clinic for hiccup. Other
times it would shoot off like sputnik—fiiiiom! That was
when I got it worst of all—Fai fai fai fai! You wey no fit
walka na fly you wan' fly? Ah, sometimes I wonder why I
didn't go deaf. [*He stands for a while, trying to remember*

what Kotonu's slippers are doing in his hands.] Where did I get these . . . Oh yes, you walk about the floor in your bare feet. If you step on a coin let me know. I know I wouldn't feel a thing.

[*Kotonu goes back to his work. Samson continues to search. Enter Salubi with guguru wrapped in paper. Like one who is accustomed to this, he cups his hands in anticipation.*]

PROF. [*as he takes the parcel.*]: Is it good? Soft? Crisp?

SALUBI: The best sir. I buy it from the usual woman.

PROF. [*examining the wrapping of the parcel.*]: That Tapa creature is a genius. She never lets me down. [*Without looking into the parcel, he empties the contents in Salubi's hands, who bows gratefully, joins the thugs and they talk in whispers. Professor smoothes out the paper itself and proceeds to read it, turns to the hand-lens, makes notes and underlines sections.*] Economic. Almost stingy. But there are the cabalistic signs. The trouble is to find the key. Find the key and it leads to the Word . . . very strange . . . very strange . . . a rash of these signs arrived lately . . . that woman of Tapa knows something, or else she is an unconscious medium. Oh God, Oh God, the enormity of unknown burdens, of hidden wisdoms . . . say the Word in our time O Lord, utter the hidden Word. [*With sudden explosiveness.*] But what do these mean? These signs were made by no human hands. What in the power of hell do they mean!

SAMSON [*coming closer and looking over Professor's shoulder.*]: I think they are pools Professor.

PROF.: I beg your pardon.

SAMSON: Football pools sir. Pools. Don't you ever play pools?

PROF.: I have little time for games.

SAMSON: No no sir. It is no game. You can make your fortune on it quite easily.

PROF. [*studies him with new interest.*]: You are a strange creature my friend. You cannot read, and I presume you cannot write, but you can unriddle signs of the Scheme that baffle even me, whose whole life is devoted to the study of the enigmatic Word? Do you actually make this modest claim for yourself?

SAMSON [*wearily*.]: Professor, I am claiming nothing. Look. Somebody has filled it up and thrown it away. You see it? It's all filled up—at least it looks like it. A cross here, or as the Tax Collector would say—Mr. Samson, his Mark. And then a lot of O here and there. That is how to fill a football coupon.

PROF.: Is that so?

SAMSON: Oh yes sir. Now here . . . this is where you write your name. You write it for me. Just put Samson there.

PROF.: You are a brave man. You would dare this in your name?

SAMSON: Please sir, just write my name. I will spell it for you— Sa-mu-son. [*The Professor writes, shrugging.*] Have you written the address?

PROF.: You have an address too?

SAMSON: The police always wrote—No fixed address. You may do the same. No, no, write . . . Samson, Apprentice Driver to Kotonu, LE 2539, NO DANGER NO DELAY— Everybody knows No Danger No Delay. No, I forget, somebody else is driving No Danger now. So perhaps you'd better write, hm, let's see . . . [*Professor throws down the pen and pushes the form aside but Samson does not notice.*] . . . yes all right, write Care of Accident Supply Store, Professor's Bar. You never know in this world. I will post it. After all, it is an asset—to use your own word now. A friend of mine—he was a messenger—sent in one of these. He won thirteen thousand. Now he owns half the houses in Apapa and they have made him a Senator. You never know you see. If I won something I will put it on a new lorry, put Kotonu to drive it. Mind you, I am not looking for thirteen thousand or anything like that. Ten thousand will do me—one must not be too greedy. Even five thousand is no child's purse-money . . . Just think, look at it on the newspaper—Samson the Champion Agbero wins five thousand.

KOTONU: I think I am standing on a penny.

SAMSON [*rushing there.*]: What did I say? If it was I, I could have that penny buried in my feet and I would not feel it. [*Picks it up.*] And a penny it is you know. I mean, it could have been a shilling, but his feet told him it was a penny. That is really how to press your accelerator.

KOTONU: Do you think something may have happened to Murano?

PROF.: What can happen to Murano? A shadow in the valley of the shadow of! Are you so conceited that you spare your concern for him?

[*A short silence. Samson sidles up to the Professor.*]

SAMSON: Professor.

PROF.: En-hm.

SAMSON: May I ask you something? A little personal?

PROF.: Why not? Even God submits himself to a weekly interrogation.

SAMSON: Thank you sir. Now, it is only as a matter of interest. You mustn't be offended sir, because I really want to know. I mean . . . is it true . . . that is, what I want to find out is . . .

PROF.: In short, you want to know whether people are right when they say I am mad.

SAMSON: No sir, certainly not. What I wanted to know is . . . well, you used to read the lesson in English in that church and we all used to enjoy your performance. In fact I don't mind telling you that you inspired many of us to start attending private classes. I was on that wall—and Kotonu

too—the day it crashed to the ground. But what has
puzzled me is this, because you see I can't stand it when
people—I don't want to mention names—when they make
nasty remarks about it—I mean, did you have a source of
private income. What I mean is Professor, what really
happened about the er . . . you know . . . this matter of
church funds?

PROF.: Sins and wages wages and sin—[*Stops. Turns and faces the
church.*] If you could see through that sealed church window
you will see the lectern bearing the Word on bronze. I stood
often behind the bronze wings of the eagle; on the broad
span of the eagle's outstretched wings rested the Word—
oh what a blasphemy it all was but I did not know it. Oh
yes, I stood then on the other side of that window—then it
was always open, not barred and bolted as it now is, from
fear—[*Samson blinks hard, rubs his eyes.*]—through that
window, my sight led straight on to this spot. In my
youth, let me tell you, in my youth we went out and waged
a holy war on every sore as this. We pulled down every
drinking shack and set fire to it, drove out the poisoners of
men's brains.

SAMSON [*spiritedly.*]: And they didn't fight back? You try that
here and see what happens to you.

PROF.: Oh the Word is a terrible fire and we burned them by the
ear. Only that was not the Word you see, oh no, it was not.
And so for every dwelling that fell ten more rose in its place
until they grew so bold that one grew here, setting its
laughter against the very throat of the organ pipes. Every
evening, until I thought, until one day I thought, I have
never really known what lies beyond that window. And
one night, the wall fell down, I heard the laughter of
children and the wall fell down in an uproar of flesh and
dust. And I left the Word hanging in the coloured light of

sainted windows. . . . [*Almost humbly*.] As you will notice,
I have made certain alterations. That corner was not there
before. I have scraped the walls. Installed an electric light.
Red neon. It is, I think, likely that I left the church coffers
much depleted . . . but I remember little of this. Have you
heard anything?

SAMSON: Oh no.

PROF.: Like your friend, I wished to retire into business. My
pension would have sufficed but since I was sacked for
blasphemy I was due for none. I forget now how much it
was, it is so difficult to remember details. Do you know
this is the only house of rest from which you can see into
the altar? But still, the business of the church funds addles
my thoughts.

SAMSON: Well you must have a clear conscience or you would
have run away.

PROF. [*mildly*.]: Run away? But I must be near the eagle, for his
brazen image bore on its back the first illusion of the Word.
Nevertheless they cast me from grace. And of all the
windows of that church, only that is kept shut.
[*Confidentially*.] You see, they know I am always watching,
watching and waiting, waiting for the careless moment, so
they keep jealous guard over the Word.

SAMSON [*looking*.]: But Professor, all the windows are open.
Even the ones up the tower.

PROF. [*cautioning with a wagging finger*.]: Be careful. They weave
a strong spell over human eyes.

SAMSON: Oh no. I can see all right. The window is wide open. I
was here this morning when the organist opened it for
practice.

PROF.: Have you sold your soul for money? You lie like a
prophet.

SAMSON: But it is the truth Professor.

PROF.: Truth? Truth? Truth my friend, is scum risen on the froth of wine.

SAMSON: All right all right, have it your own way.
[*Continues to cast glances at the window.*]

PROF.: Do let me know if you hear anything . . . about the matter of the church funds.

SAMSON: I would forget about it if I were you. They would have done something by now if they wanted to.

PROF.: The dust in the belfry never quite settles. It only awaits the next clangour of the bell. Come closer . . . closer . . .
[*Samson with obvious reluctance, obeys. Professor draws down his head sharply, whispers piercingly in his ear.*] Be like a bat. Keep your ears stuck to the vestry door. If I lose the station all is lost. I must watch what they do. I must see what goes on at the altar, at the pulpit. And you watch with me . . . see that no changes are made without my permission.

SAMSON [*struggling to get free.*]: Yes sir, yes sir . . .

PROF.: Up the aisle with them and into the chancel. Don't let their cassock deter you, the eagle sides with me. We will do battle, but first we must find the Word . . .

SAMSON: Oh yes sir, of course Professor.

PROF.: For the day will come, oh yes it will. Even atonement wilts before the Word . . .
[*Samson breaks free with desperate strength, flees up-stage only to be met by the explosive fall of the tailboard. Right on the sound the light changes, leaving only the store area in light. Falling grotesquely after the board, is the mask. A moment later, Kotonu emerges from behind the mass of junk and clothing. Immediately, the mask-followers fill the stage searching for their mask-bearer. Kotonu stands dazed but Samson quickly raises the board and pushes the mask under it. It is a Drivers' festival and they are all armed with whips and thick fibre stalks. Two carry a dog tied to a stake and brandish*]

matchets. *Dashing everywhere with the steady leader-and-refrain chant they break off sporadically for brief mutual whipping contests, dashing off again in pursuit.*]

SAMSON [*as soon as they disappear.*]: Help me lift him on board.

KOTONU: You saw it. Nothing could have saved him.

SAMSON: Come on come on.

KOTONU: It's all your fault. You said we should come.

SAMSON: That is neither here nor there. Let's hide him before they return.

KOTONU: But it wasn't my fault. Nothing could have saved him.

SAMSON: For heaven's sake man help me carry him up.

KOTONU: You know my reflexes are good Samson, but the way he ran across . . .

SAMSON: They'll be back this way again.

KOTONU: But what was he running from? It was almost as if he was determined to die. Like those wilful dogs getting in the way of the wheels.

SAMSON: I am not the police Kotonu. Neither are those people. They talk with matchets. Across the throats—matchets!

KOTONU: Did you ask me here to be their butcher? You saw him, the way he fled across. Just tell me, was I to be part of this?

SAMSON [*manhandles the figure into the lorry and replaces the tailboard.*]: Now get in and START THE ENGINE!

KOTONU: It's probably stalled.

SAMSON: What kind of talk is that? Have you gone mad? You haven't even tried man.

KOTONU: But it wasn't my fault.

SAMSON [*peers into the distance.*]: They are coming again. Kotonu, for the last time!

KOTONU: Let me look underneath the mask.

SAMSON: Have you gone mad . . . too late anyway, they've filled the road. But run at least. Come on let's run!

KOTONU: But who is he? Why did he run across?

SAMSON: You're hopeless. [*Hurriedly he pulls down the tarpaulin.*] But at least don't give us away. Look as if we are part of the festival. If there is danger one of us will have to get inside the mask. Do you understand?

[*Dumbly, Kotonu nods. The maskers come in again, performing the dance of the whips, darting off again and back, looking for the missing god.*

One of them dashes suddenly to the lorry and lifts up the tarpaulin. With desperate speed Samson snatches a whip from the nearest person and gives him a cut across the legs. The man readily accepts the invitation, and a contest follows.]

SAMSON [*shouts above the din.*]: Now Kotonu, now! [*Kotonu hesitates, visibly frightened.*] Kotonu! Strip the mask and get under it! Kotonu it's the only way.

[*As if suddenly wakened, Kotonu starts, climbs into the lorry. The whip-dance grows fast and furious. Samson manoeuvres himself near the tailboard from time to time.*] Hurry Kotonu! For heaven's sake hurry!

[*There is a sudden violent movement against the canvas and Samson, scared, rushes there. Almost at the same time, the masquerade comes through in violent throes, a figure in torment. There is a loud yell from the dancers and the whipping and chanting becomes more violent, aiding the god's seeming possession.*]

KOTONU [*tearing at the clothes, demented.*]: It's all wet inside, I've got his blood all over me. [*They dance and whip one another around the masquerade, leaving a clear space for his frenzy.*] It's getting dark Samson I can't see. His blood has got in my eyes. I can't see Samson. [*Samson, wildly irresolute, battles on with his latest challenger.*] Samson where are you? My eyes are all clammed up I tell you. Samson! Samson! Samson!

[*His struggles become truly frantic, full of violent contortions. Gradually he grows weaker and weaker, collapsing slowly on the ground until he is completely inert. The dancers flog one another off the scene.*

A slow black-out, and a half-minute pause.

They are all back to normal. Enter Particulars Joe.]

PARTIC. JOE: Did he come in here?

SAMSON [*turns away with undisguised boredom.*]: No, he went the other way.

PARTIC. JOE: Are you sure?

SAMSON: Am I sure about what?

PARTIC. JOE: That he went the other way. I could have sworn I saw him come in here.

SAMSON: Nobody came in here.

PARTIC. JOE: Are you sure you know who I mean? Sort of tall but a little on the short side. Tribal marks, but beginning to wear off . . . in fact, unless you looked closely you might think he had no tribal marks at all. Rather light in complexion, mind you it's a bit dark in here, so you could easily think him a somewhat darkish fellow. He was wearing a huge agbada but then, he could have shed it while I was chasing him.

SAMSON: Who are you chasing today?

PARTIC. JOE [*coming in fully.*]: Well, it is the usual trouble you know. A hit-and-run-driver.

KOTONU: Is the victim dead?

PARTIC. JOE: I had no time to find out.

KOTONU: You were so determined to catch him you left the body!

PARTIC. JOE: Oh no, the suspect himself took care of that. You see, he collided against a goat.

SAMSON: Ho ho ho, you really are full of surprises. So it's a goat today.

KOTONU: And you are chasing the man for colliding with a
　　　　goat?

PARTIC. JOE: Well you see, he stopped . . .

SAMSON: You said just now he did not stop.

PARTIC. JOE: Oh he didn't stop. That is, he stopped you see. He
　　　　picked up the goat and then ran off with it. Just think of
　　　　that. The next thing you know they'll all be running off
　　　　with mortuary claims. [*Looking at Kotonu.*] You wouldn't
　　　　know anything about that sort of thing would you?

PROF. [*without looking up from his work, after a nervous silence.*]:
　　　　Why don't you sit down a while officer. You must be
　　　　tired from all this running around, and Murano will soon
　　　　be here. [*Looks towards the church window.*] They ought to
　　　　light up before long. [*Brings out the watch.*] The organist is
　　　　rinsing his dirty face in cold water. The pastor is fixing his
　　　　borrowed collar-stud. And the communicants are beating
　　　　their husbands.

PARTIC. JOE: Well I really ought to go after this suspect . . .

PROF.: Later later, he won't get away. Do sit down.

PARTIC. JOE: That is very kind of you sir, very kind of you. I
　　　　could do with a rest to tell the truth.

SAMSON: God! All this pretence. He knows very well why he
　　　　comes here. Somehow he always chases his suspects here
　　　　at this time of the day.

PROF.: Tolerance. Tolerance my friend. There will be enough
　　　　for everyone. Enough to breed unawareness which you all
　　　　seek in your futile ways.

SAMSON: Well I don't mind the others, but him . . . hey just a
　　　　minute.
　　　　[*Particulars, about to sit down, sees a coin in a floor crack and is
　　　　transfering it into his pocket. Samson runs across and snatches it.*]
　　　　That happens to be mine.

PARTIC. JOE [*blandly.*]: That's O.K. Natural mistake on my part.

Money has been left for me in more unlikely places believe
me.

SAMSON: Well at least wait until I am back on the road before
you collect tolls.

[*Particulars folds his arms and waits.*]

PROF.: How is the criminal world my friend?

PARTIC. JOE: More lucrative every day Professor.

PROF.: Not for the criminal I trust.

PARTIC. JOE: Oh no sir. That would only corrupt them.

[*A brief silence, Samson has gone to look at the spiders, he
keeps poking the web gently with a stick.*]

PARTIC. JOE: I haven't seen your hand on the roads lately
Professor.

PROF.: I am slowing down. I have to cut down on distractions.
I need all my strength for uncovering the Word. Forgery
saps my powers.

PARTIC. JOE: Do let us know when you retire. It will be a great
load off our minds. We spend more time separating your
own handiwork than we do in detecting the general
forgery. We would be so sorry to make a mistake.

PROF.: I would be too. And yet it might not be such a bad idea.

PARTIC. JOE: I beg your pardon sir.

PROF.: I spend much time considering it. Too many people come
to me for help. They depend on me and I find I am
reluctant to let them down. That worm over there for
instance, he is awaiting a document. These two tormented
devils are my patients. Other people's sorrows sap my
energy and these days, it is not so easy to be deaf. A spell in
prison might help me. Conserve my scattered energies.

PARTIC. JOE: You will be disillusioned Professor. Prison is the
least solitary community in the world.

PROF.: I will insist on being difficult. Then the warders will
punish me with solitary confinement.

PARTIC. JOE: The food is terrible.

PROF.: Just bread and water. That would not be asking much, plain bread and water.

PARTIC. JOE: Well, y-y-yes it might work. Taken that way it might work.

PROF.: I know it will.

PARTIC. JOE [*after much hemming*.]: Professor, I . . . er . . . hate to appear to be self-seeking, but after all sir, you are a man of the world and you will understand my position I trust. I mean Professor, I have been, you will admit, very co-operative and loyal . . .

PROF.: Stop worrying your head officer. I promise you no other person will have the credit of arresting me.

PARTIC. JOE [*vastly relieved*.]: Thank you sir, thank you very much. That is something to look forward to.
[*Samson spits on the ground, turns his back on him.*]

PROF.: Charity my friend, charity. [*To Particulars*.] I will let you know when it is time. When a man retires he must be able to retire somewhere. I look forward to contemplation in solitude.

SALUBI [*leaping up suddenly*.]: Murano!

PROF.: Sit down you fool. Murano makes no sound.
[*Enter Say Tokyo Kid.*]

SAY T. [*looks round a little worriedly*.]: I ain't late am I?

SALUBI: Say Tokyo! Say Tokyo Kid!

SAY T.: Salubi Salubirity! Say man, everybody garrered round the goorold place. How's business kid?

SALUBI: Say Tokyo Charranooga Shoe-Shine Boy!

SAY T.: Thas me. I'm allright boy. [*Sees the officer and recoils. Makes to pull an imaginary gun from his belt*.]
Whas that guy doing around here?

SAMSON: Say Tokyo!

SAY T.: I say boy it sure is good to be back among friendly faces.

Goorold Samson the Champion Tout! And Kotonu the
demon driver himself, coast-to-coast Dakar to Yola Koton
Kafiri to Kontagora No Danger No Delay Here Today
Gone Tomorrow. How's business kid?

SAMSON: Moving moving on greased wheels thank heavens.
[*Say Tokyo looks at his men with prolonged contempt and they
slink further and further into the corner.*]

SAY T.: You see rem? If Ah'd been butchered and chopped in a
thousand pieces they wouldn't have been able to tell what
happened to me. Tell me Samson, ain't they already making
dirge for Say Tokyo Kid? They sure goor a that sorta
thing.

SAMSON: What happened Tokyo? They all looked as if you
were ... well, outnumbered.

THUG: We never got to the fight. The road played us foul. A
tree had fallen across the road and our driver didn't see it in
time.

SAY T.: Yeah sure. And none of you cares to finrout what
become of your Cap'n.

THUG: Well we looked. You had disappeared.

SAY T.: You think a man disappears in the middle of the road
without cause? There was no river, it wasn't on a bridge so
you couldn't say I had been washed away.

THUG: But Say Tokyo, you simply vanished.

SAY T.: Because ah was off in pursuit of the murderers you
damned cowards. That tree didn't fall by itself. It was
knocked across the road. I was sirring in front so ah saw the
gang just before we turned the corner and hit the tree.

THUG: Well we were in no shape for chasing anyone.

SAY T.: They weren't in no shape for standing up against we
either? They thought they killed us when the truck
sommersaulted. Man they just turn tail and fled. And you
were so full of self-pity you didn't even wait to finrout. I

could have been chopped to pieces in that bush and no
one would remember ah existed.

THUG: Well, we didn't know.

SAY T.: God, don't you know yer Cap'n? You think I can just
disappear like that?

SALUBI: Say Tokyo Kid!

SAY T.: That's me. You know I drive nothing but timber. Are
you so godless that you think a little timber across the road
would finish me?

PARTIC. JOE [*who has been making notes.*]: Has this accident been
reported? Or any other accident. Has anyone anything to
declare? You know the regulations.

SAY T.: That ain't ma business.

PARTIC. JOE: Give me the particulars.

SAY T.: If you wanre pareculars you go in that bush and dig
inside the sommersaulted truck. I ain't re driver.

PARTIC. JOE: I take it No Casualty?

SAY T.: There may be one if you don't quit asking me questions.

PARTIC. JOE [*moving towards Professor.*]: Sir, if I may use a
little portion of your assembly time . . . since our beloved
Murano is not yet here sir . . .

PROF.: What for officer?

PARTIC. JOE: On investigation sir. Unreported accident Suspicion
of foul play and accesories before and after the fact.

PROF.: Be careful. [*Spoken mildly, and he turns and resumes his
work.*]

PARTIC. JOE [*saluting smartly.*]: Very kind of you sir. We shall of
course look forward to returning the compliment. [*Whips
round sharply to Kotonu in dramatic-interrogator pose.*] Where
were you the day of the Drivers' Festival? On the Feast of
Ogun the dog-eater. Where?

KOTONU: Where?

PARTIC. JOE: Answer me—where? And I hereby warn you that

anything you say or do will be taken and used in evidence et cetera et cetera. Speak up where were you?

SAMSON: Come to that where were you yourself?

PARTIC. JOE: I don't fancy dogs.

SAY T.: A spy! I always reckoned I couldn't trust that guy.

PARTIC. JOE: On investigation. Duty before friendship. Were you at the Festival of Drivers? Account for your movements.

PROF. [not looking up.]: Was that the day of the miracle officer?

PARTIC. JOE: It was the day a god was abducted Professor.

PROF.: Abducted?

SAY T. [rising.]: My wife's brother was there.

PARTIC. JOE: Eye-witnesses only I said. No housewives' gossips etcetera.

THE GANG: That's good enough . . .
    He's an eye-witness . . .
    I saw him there . . .
    His wife's brother is acceptable . . .
    You police are all the same . . .
    Taking bribes is all you know . . .

SAY T.: Now you look here officer, you trying to insult ma family?

PARTIC. JOE: All right all right, you're an eye-witness. Speak on. [Nods and mumbles of approval.]

SAY T.: It was after all, our own festival, so I don't reckon it's any of your business what happened to the guest of honour that day. [Cheers.] 's far as we git the marrer, Ogun came among us in possession before their very. . . .

GANG: We saw it. We all saw it.

SAY T.: Before our own very eyes. And surrenly, he vanished. Surrenly he vanished. Ain't gor nuthin' more to say. And you also can now close up that notebook of yours and—suddenly—vanish!

[*Prolonged cheers.*]

PARTIC. JOE: Well that may be good enough for you but it isn't good enough for . . .

KOTONU: If I may say something . . .

GANG: Shurrup . . .

Case closed . . .

To hell with policeman . . .

Ogun break all den head. . . .

KOTONU [*going down to the Professor.*]: Professor, I never even saw his face . . .

[*Particulars trails him, note-book at the ready. Professor pays no attention.*]

We drove down all night. We dared not wait Professor, the sacrificial knives of those men were right at our backs. . . . We parked the lorry outside here with the dead man in it. We were waiting for you to come, we couldn't think what to do. Well, by morning the body was gone. . . .

PARTIC. JOE [*scribbling furiously.*]: What body? What body?

KOTONU: Only the mask was left Professor. The body was gone.

PARTIC. JOE: Tangible evidence, the mask. Where is it?

[*The Gang tries singing to counter their voices. The pace of action is rapid.*]

SAMSON [*at the top of his lungs.*]: Where the hell is that Murano?

PARTIC. JOE: I beg to apply for a search warrant. Compliment to be returned at the very earliest opportunity.

[*Professor waves him on. He turns and dives into the store.*]

SAMSON: That's private property. [*Tries to bar his way.*]

PARTIC. JOE: In the name of the law!

[*Reaches a hand into the store towards the mask. Say Tokyo pulls his cap down his face and Samson quickly substitutes a military uniform so that the policeman's hand grabs this. The mask is then taken out and thrown from one person to the other until it is hidden under the Professor's chair. Particulars*]

frees his eyes, clutching the uniform triumphantly.]
Concrete evidence of tangible evidence—what's this!

SAMSON [*his hands across his chest, dolefully.*]: Poor Sergeant
Burma.

THE GANG [*with equal solemnity.*]: Poor Sergeant Burma.
[*Samson takes the uniform, puts it on.*]

PARTIC. JOE: I say, that's Sergeant Burma's uniform. I'd know
it anywhere.

SAY T.: You mean you knew old Sergeant Burma?

PARTIC. JOE: Knew him? We were at the front together. Lifelong
friends me and Burma. Told him to come into the police
force, but oh no, he preferred his wretched motor transport.

SAMSON: Only fools drive oil tankers. They are clumsy monsters.

PARTIC. JOE [*reminiscing, sentimental.*]: He loved them. Oloibiri
to Lagos. Port Harcourt to Kano. And he always said,
God bless the oil companies for bringing out my genius.
And he drove his tanker like a tank. Of course he was huge
himself, like his truck.

SAMSON: Till the tanker did for him.

PARTIC. JOE: There was little wrong with the end of Sergeant
Burma. He went up in a pyre that would have honoured
Sango himself. Such a big man. He had to crouch in the
driver's cabin.

SAMSON: And a voice like a referee's whistle . . . [*mimicking.*]
You see this monster . . . that is nothing. I drive bigger
tanks in Burma campaign. I drive supply caravans, and I
turn-turn this picken with one hand. Na picken 'e be. Na
small picken. You wan' try? You tink say na every Tom
Dick and Harry fit drive tanker? My friend, me na veteran
driver.

PARTIC. JOE: Every year on Rememberance Day, over in that
church, he put that on. And I had mine plus a Long Service
ribbon. It is peaceful to fight a war which one does not

understand, to kill human beings who never seduced your
wife or poisoned your water. Sapele to Burma—that was a
long way for a quarrel.

SAMSON [*gives a quick act of polish to the medals. Sticks out his
chest. Assumes full military bearing.*]: You think I get these
medals for nothing? They wan' give me the King George
Cross self, but you know how things be for blackman. My
major recommend me for the decoration but dey begin
ask how den go give black man dat kind honour? Another
time the general send cablegram wit' in own hand. 'E say,
gi'am Victoria Cross. I say make you gi'am, blackman or
no blackman—gi'am. Dey for give me dat one but when
the governor for home hear wetin dey wan' do, 'e cable
back say if den give me dat kind superior medal, I go return
my country begin do political agitator. Haba! Justice no
dey for white man world.

PARTIC. JOE: Sergeant Burma survived four years of fighting and
one year as a prisoner of war. . . .

SAMSON: Den beat me so tey my backside dey like dat Zeppelin
balloon. If you put pin for am 'e go burs'.

PARTIC. JOE: On Rememberance day all the big shots were
present and our Professor here read the lesson in his
sonorous tones while the bishop preached a moving
sermon, and Sergeant Burma sang five notes behind the
congregation who sang three notes behind the choir who
sang two notes behind the organ. . . .
[*Strains of a 'rememberance' hymn, the four sections ending in
that order, one after the other, Sergeant Burma last of all, singing
'Africa' style and a prolonged A-a-men to boot. During which . . .*]
Burma, Burma, congregation done finish long time.

SAMSON [*in the same falsetto, jabbing Particulars savagely with the
elbow.*]: Lef' me! I say make you lef' me. Wetin be my
concern for dat one? I no care whether the Governor and

in aide-de-camp finish de same hymn since yesterday. Na
dey go fight for Burma? I tink say dis Rememberance Day
na for we own countryman wey die for combat. [*Turning
round the other way.*] Shurrup yourself. I say make you
shurrup yourself. Na so we dey sing am for army camp and
if you no like am make you commot for church go talk
Latin for Catholic church.

PARTIC. JOE: We were made much of in those days. To have
served in Burma was to have passed your London Matric.
Sergeant Burma looked forward to retirement and his
choice of business came as a matter of course. . . . and
Professor offered him the business corner of the drivers'
haven . . . the Accident Corner.

SAMSON: Wetin enh? Wetin? You tink say myself I no go die
some day? When person die, 'e done die and dat one done
finish. I beg, if you see moto accident make you tell me.
We sabbee good business . . . sell spare part and second-hand
clothes. Wetin? You tink say I get dat kind sentimentation?
Me wey I done see dead body so tey I no fit chop meat
unless den cook am to nonsense? Go siddon my friend.
Business na business. If you see accident make you tell me
I go run go there before those useless men steal all the spare
part finish.

PARTIC. JOE: Sergeant Burma looked forward to retiring and
doing the spare part business full-time. But of course his
brakes failed going down a hill. . . .

[*The group begins to dirge, softly as if singing to themselves. A
short silence. Samson's face begins to show horror and he gasps
as he realizes what he has been doing.*]

SAMSON [*tearing off the clothes.*]: God forgive me! Oh God,
forgive me. Just see, I have been fooling around pretending
to be a dead man. Oh God I was only playing I hope you
realize. I was only playing.

PARTIC. JOE: Such a fire ... such a fire. ... Nothing but black twigs left of the veteran of the Burma campaign ... I went to break the news to his wife. You know what she said?

SAMSON: No no, talk of something else I beg you.

PARTIC. JOE: She said, I always told him not to gather dead men's wallets. And she was coming here to set fire to the whole store.

PROF.: Set fire to my store!

PARTIC. JOE: That's what I told her. Maybe the goods belong to your husband I said, but the idea was Professor's.

PROF.: A spiritual ownership—more important than the material.

SAMSON: I wish she'd burnt the whole place.

PARTIC. JOE: She wasn't going to burn his money though. Oh Sergeant Burma was a rich man. He searched the pockets before the police or the ambulance came. Looting was after all the custom in the front. You killed your enemy and you robbed him. He couldn't break the habit.

SAMSON: But this is not war.

PROF.: Liar. Even these rags [*waving a newspaper*] understand its nature. Like a battlefield they always say. Like a battlefield.

SAMSON: Oh well, they all caught up with him. People don't do that sort of thing and get away with it.

PARTIC. JOE: Are you getting superstitious in your old age Samson?

SAMSON [*desperately to Kotonu.*]: You should never have touched the stuff.

KOTONU: Why not? Much more peaceful to trade in death than to witness it.

PARTIC. JOE [*recollecting.*]: Hoi hoi hoi! You bloody dealer in death—Where were you on the day of the Drivers' Festival?

SAMSON: Speak to the Professor. He handles everything for us.

SAY T. [*derisively.*]: That's gorrim. Well whar you wairing for? Ain't you gonna interrogate the Professor?

[*They push and egg him on, forming a semi-circle behind him.*]

PARTIC. JOE: Sir ... at the suggestion of these hangers-on of yours ... thinking sir, that as a man who wanders on the roads quite a bit and picks up significant events which would escape the ordinary eye, we were wondering sir, if you may chance to have er ... discovered something which ... er ... might be able to assist the police in their investigations.... Sir.

PROF.: May an ignorant man ask what god you pretend to worship?

PARTIC. JOE: Same as the other sir, the road.

SAMSON [*whispering.*]: Professor, don't forget I paid my consultation fee....

PARTIC. JOE: Any assistance sir ... the compliment will be repaid, that's an official guarantee.

PROF.: It is true I am a gleaner, I dare not be swayed by marvels. Stick to the air and to open earth, wet my feet in morning dew, gleaning loose words from the road. Remain with the open eye of earth until the shadow of the usurping word touches my place of exile. But I broke my habit. I succumbed to the flaunting of a single word, forgot that exercise of spirit which demands that I make daily pilgrimage in search of leavings. I deserted my course, and —rightly—I lost my way. That was the vengeance of the Word. [*His manner changes gradually, becomes more deliberate, emphatic, like someone giving a lecture. And they listen, attentive, as if to a customary lesson in their daily routine.*] But don't we all change from minute to minute? If we didn't we wouldn't hope to die. Well, same as the road. My favourite paths are those trickles among green fastnesses, on which whole forests are broken up—between the falling dew and the evening mists the nature of those paths changes right beneath my feet. But I am set in my ways—I should have followed my daily route. [*Turns in his chair, half-facing them.*] I pick my words only among rejects. [*He pats the bundles.*] You must have observed it. But I have no new finds to show you today because today was my day of error. I wandered on my favourite roads as usual, but I had not the courage to pick them up where they lay, stray and neglected. That word which I plucked early in the day was full-bellied, it was a robust growth, well-nourished, stout and pithy. And in my foolish excitement I uprooted it and bore it off, a trophy from the war. For my blindness I missed my way. I suppose I should ask your forgiveness for claiming pacts with words which grow above my station. My task is to keep company with the fallen, and this word rose in pride above spiked bushes. We must all stick together. Only the fallen have need of restitution. [*He turns round to his table, waves them off.*] Call out the hymn. Any song will do but to restore my self-confidence make it a song of praise. But mind you don't disturb me. I feel like working.

[*Falls straight on his papers as the group sings his favourite praise-song.*]

Professor anjonnu t'awa
Professor anjonnu t'awa
Baba wa l'oke baba
Baba wa l'odo baba
Eni ba ma a gbe mi san'le, ko da'wo duro
Mo leni lehin, ejo ragbada l'ori awo
A y'awo pada, ejo ragbada l'ori awo
Ota o lef'ori omo baba gun'yan je
A b'oro soro a b'elerigbo b'okele
Baba wa l'oke baba

Baba wa l'odo baba. . . .

[*As they sing, Professor gives short, cynical laughs. Then he turns round suddenly, vicious contempt in his voice, and they stop.*]

PROF.: If you think I do this from the kindness of my heart you are fools. But you are no fools, so you must be liars. It is true I demand little from you, just your presence at evening communion, and the knowledge you afford me that your deaths will have no meaning. Well look at you, battered in pieces and I ask no explanation. I let you serve two masters, three, four, five, a hundred if you wish. But understand that I would live as hopefully among cattle, among hogs, among rams if it were Ramaddan, I would live as hopefully if you were ant-heaps destined to be crushed underfoot. But I suppose you my friend, would dare to call this also, accident?

KOTONU: Professor, I haven't said anything.

PROF.: Not you. Your friend. But I thank you all who hasten the redeeming of the Word. You are important I promise you. Everyone here is important. Your lives whittle down the last obstacle to the hidden Word.

PARTIC. JOE [*turning back sheets in his notebook.*]: In that case sir, perhaps we will be of mutual assistance to each other. Our investigations indicate that the man who was possessed at the Festival of Drivers was a palm wine tapper by trade. The coincidence involved will be of great interest to my bosses, but I am, as you know sir, a humble man and very approachable.

SAY T.: Hey, wairaminute wairaminute . . .

SAMSON: Kotonu, did you hear that?

PARTIC. JOE: Professor sir, have you anything to say?

PROF.: Remember my warning. Be careful I said. Be careful. If my enemies trouble me I shall counter with a resurrection.

Capital R. I shall set up shop in full opposition—I have the advantage.

PARTIC. JOE: Is that your last word Professor?

PROF.: That is my message. [*Brings out his watch.*] And now Murano should arrive. But remember my warning. [*Footsteps approaching.*]

KOTONU: Somebody is coming.

[*Say Tokyo spins round, imaginary pistol at the draw.*]

SAY T.: You just stay right there and don't move.

Enter Murano, bearing a large, outsize gourd. White froth topped. Say T. gives a huge leap in the air, tosses the 'gun' in the air. Catches and fires several shots in all directions. General relaxation and hum of contentment.]

PROF. [*looks at his watch.*]: On time as usual my boy. Welcome. [*Murano sets down the gourd beside him, prostrates. Goes inside to fetch a variety of bowls and calabash cups. There is a very elegant glass for Professor which he polishes carefully. Professor examines the finished job through his monocle, Murano spills a libation to earth. Then they sit with their eyes on the Prof. awaiting a signal. A few moments, and lights appear through the stained glass windows.*]

PROF.: Hearken! [*First softly, gradually building up, the sound of organ music.*] Observe the saintly progress of the evening communicants! [*Organ music continues.*] Note, [*pointing to the glass window*] I hold nothing against the rainbow, considering it to be good. I hold nothing against lights, against colour, finding in it mists and fragments of the Imminent grace on earth. But I said . . . I mean, I only sought to make my meaning clear, and I could not escape the source of my own sense of wonder . . . God! He called it blasphemy.

[*Murano pours palm wine for everybody.*]

What if they were children? Is truth ever to be hidden

from children? Yes, what though there was the spirit of
wine upon me. It was Sunday, Palm Sunday and each child
bore a cross of the tender frond, yellow and green against
their innocence. What I said, I did not deny. . . .

[*He begins to chuckle in spite of himself the moment he holds out
the glass.*]

You should have seen his face, oh you should have seen
his glory face! He was such a busybody that bishop, and it
was his just reward for sneaking up on me during Sunday
School. . . . What are you doing teacher he said? I turned,
and there behind me stood the figure of judgement. Why,
explaining the lesson of the rainbow to my pupils. And
how, he asked, did I hear you explain it just now? So I
told him, very gently. . . . Child, I said, my dear child,
God painted the sign of the rainbow, a promise that the
world shall not perish from floods. Just as he also carved
the symbol of the palm, a covenant that the world shall not
perish from thirst.

[*Loud laughter, dying off gradually to a silence which is again
gradually filled by organ music. Professor listens for some
moments, then turns to the band.*]

Wipe out that sound, God forgive them.

[*Murano refills his glass, squats on the floor beside him. The
band begins playing, drowning the organ music almost at once.
When a cup is emptied, the owner summons Murano, who refills
it. The singing runs freely, uninhibited. Say Tokyo Kid is
obviously recounting his adventures, especially to Salubi.
Professor resumes his studies.*]

SAY T. [*his voice suddenly above the din.*]: Say whas wrong wir that
kid? He sure acting funny.

[*It cuts across the noise, they mostly turn to look at Murano who
has seen the mask and lifted it out, his face working with
an effort of the mind. Kotonu has come to the table, his eyes*]

fixed on the mute, the silence reaches the Professor and he looks at them.]

PROF.: Why, my dear coast-to-coast driver, what is the matter?

KOTONU: Nothing Professor nothing.

PROF.: Is the child interested in that costume? You must remember he's a child and bright things attract him. Murano has no mind. He neither speaks nor hears nor remembers, and one leg is shorter than the other.
[*Murano, at the sound of the Professor's voice has almost begun to be afraid. About to throw aside the mask.*]

KOTONU: Professor, I asked you once . . .

PROF.: If Murano was the god-apparent?

SAMSON: And for God's sake, Professor, give a straight answer for a change.

PROF.: Murano could not reveal much, returning instinctively to his old trade, tapping wine from trees; beyond that, he had retained no further link to what he was or where he had been. That, that especially where he had been. And waiting, waiting till his tongue be released, [*desperately*] in patience and in confidence, for he is not like you others whose faces are equally blank but share no purpose with the Word. So, surely Murano, crawling out of the darkness, from the last suck of the throat of death, and Murano with the spirit of a god in him, for it came to the same thing, that I held a god captive, that his hands held out the day's communion! And should I not hope, with him, to cheat, to anticipate the final confrontation, learning its nature baring its skulking face, why may I not understand . . .
[*He stops, looks around him.*] So, why don't you ask him you runaway driver, why don't you ask him to try it on, see if it fits. . . .
[*He pulls up Murano, takes him into the store, pulls the canvas behind him.*]

Let us forget the mute one.

[*He waves to the group and they resume playing, uncertainly, afraid.*

Very slowly, a small measure of gaiety returns. But they all remain nervous, expectant.]

SAY T.: Come on, service me the stuff. [*He gives one of his men the cup.*] And hurry up cause lak a said, we'r gerring out of this joint soon. I don' reckon on staying long in re same place as that Professor guy.

[*His attention is fixed constantly on the store.*]

THUG: Cap'n....

SAY T.: Shurrup wharre hell you mean? I tell you I found their hideout. We goinra pay them a surprise visit tonight whether you lak it or you don't.

[*Samson finds himself doing a running battle with a fly. He loses eventually, the fly succeeds in landing in his wine. Samson leaps up angrily, scoops out the froth with the fly in it, and carefully takes the fly between two fingers. After a moment's thought he takes the fly to the spider's web, throws it in, and stays to watch the spider seize it, a satisfied grin spreading over his face.*]

SAMSON [*obviously slightly drunk.*]: Got him? A-ah, he understands the game all right. Easy as chucking an unwilling passenger into a lorry. I may not be an expert driver . . . in fact I must confess, I am no driver at all, got thick soles and the gear always goes in the wrong place. But one thing no one will deny . . . Salubi!

SALUBI: Wetin?

SAMSON: Say Tokyo.

SAY T. [*absently.*]: Whas cooking kid?

SAMSON: Just tell me you two. What do they call me?

SALUBI: Samson Baba Agbero.

SAMSON: Yeah boy.

SAY T.: King of Touts.

SAMSON: Na me dat. As you see me like this, I am a quiet, peace-loving man, but when we get to motor park, I don't know my brother again.

SALUBI: King of Touts! Champion of motor park!

SAMSON: I'm all right. Murano. Service me man. God bless you, man devil or whatever you are, God bless you. Murano? Where's he gone? 'E fun awon enia wonyi . . . ni oti. Yah! Go and ask of me. From Dorma-Ahenkro to Abidjan. Ask anyone who is the greatest tout of them all. Samson thas me, King of Touts.

PARTIC JOE: Samson Baba!

SAMSON: I'm all right. Ti o l'eru ese! [*Begins to demonstrate his tactics.*] Sisi! A-ah. Sisi o. Sisi wey fine reach so na only bus wey fine like we own fit carry am. Wetin now sisi? Oh your portmanteau, I done put am inside bus. Yes, certainly. We na quick service, we na senior service. A-ah mama, na you dey carry all dis load for your head? A-ah. Gentleman no dey for dis world again . . . Oya mama, we done ready for go now now; na you be de las' for enter . . . Hey, Kotonu, fire am, make am vu-um . . . oga abi you no hear? We done ready for go—no delay us at all at all. Come o, come now. Service na first class, everything provided. If you wan' pee we go stop, No delay! Wetin you dey talk? I say no delay? Which kin' policeman? Abi you know dis bus? No Delay . . . no policeman go delay us for road. This bus get six corner and we done put bribe for each corner. No nonsense no palaver. Ah, olopa, my good friend corporal, make you come join we bus now . . . look in neck, 'e done fat pon-pon-pon e done chop bribe so tey in neck dey swell like pig belle . . . oh corporal come on sir, come on for we bus sir . . . a-ah long time no see. Welcome o, how family sah, ah-ah, na you dey look so-so

thin like sugar-cane so? Abi den dey give you too much
work. Ah, o ma se o, na so policeman life be . . . hn,
onijibiti, 'e done chop bribe in face dey shine like tomato.
Ah, misisi, misisi, na you bus dey wait you here. . . .
[*From inside, the canvas is pushed aside, emerging silently, the
egungun. The laughter dies out gradually all eyes on the
apparition. One by one the hands splutter and die on the
instruments.*]

SALUBI [*trying to sneak out.*]: No one is playing around with my
sanity. I'm not staying to witness this.

PROF.: Let no one move!
[*Salubi hurriedly sits.*]

PARTIC. JOE: Professor, you know I am not superstitious. I mean,
in my position I can't afford to be. But this . . . I swear sir,
I would sooner you forged a hundred insurance policies.

PROF.: I must hope, even now. I cannot yet believe that death's
revelation must be total, or not at all.

SAY T.: I reckon this has gone too far. I ain't scared like all these
people so I'm telling you, you're fooling around where you
ain't got no business. . . . I'm Say Tokyo Kid and I don't
give you one damn!

PROF. [*explosively.*]: Do you cringe because you are confronted
by the final gate to the Word? My friends, Murano is dumb
and this creature suffers from gutturals like a love-crazed
frog and yet you let the one sustain your spirits and the
other fill you dead with awe. [*Shouting at the band.*] Play
you croakers, play! Or have the blessings of Murano's daily
pilgrimage dried already in the hollows of your cheeks?
Play and burst your flooded throats before I draw the
bowstring of the Word and the veiled shaft bores paths of
faith across your cowering mind. Do I feed you wine for
nothing? Play you foul-mouthed vermin of the road!
[*They obey him slowly, beating out the rhythm of agemo*

emerging from the bowels of earth.
He goes round with the gourd, waving aside Samson who offers
to help. The egungun continues to dance, and the group pick
up quickly when Professor approaches them.]

PROF.: I hope you will not think my gratitude excessive, but you
make me feel that I was back among my Sunday-School
children. It is a painful thing to desert one's calling—ask
your friend over there who still cannot tear himself from
the road. Following in the path of Sergeant Burma is no
substitute—he will find that out.

SAY T. [*whispers fiercely to Salubi.*]: I don't want no curse on my
head.

SALUBI: Let's not annoy him. You know how he is.

SAY T.: Annoy him! Do you want to go blind from things you
shouldn't see.

PROF.: We have after all, to decide many things, as for instance,
who next runs our store. The coast-to-coast driver is a
little tired and the regular customers have lost patience.

SAY T. [*hoarsely to Salubi.*]: I ain't afraid. Even if he's master of the
spirits of every timber I ever wrestled with, I can teach him
a lesson.

PROF. [*filling Samson's cup.*]: It is not in my nature to be trusting.
Human beings, even such as you prove so tenacious, and
I have despaired again and again. But I hope you will
remember that we formed a syndicate.

SAMSON: I had forgotten all that business Professor.

PROF.: So I cannot desert you. I only hope, whoever it is, that
you will not balk me, that you will not keep me waiting
until I am beyond benefiting from our settlement. . . .
One must cheat fear, by fore-knowledge.
[*They all keep their eyes on him, with varying reactions, mostly*
fear. The egungun continues to dance, Professor to
dispense the drink.]

I feel powered tonight, but that is usual. But I also feel at last a true excitement of the mind and spirit. As if that day has been lowered at last which I have long awaited. Surely I am not alone. If I am that, then I have wasted evenings of instruction on you. [*Mildly, almost with tiredness.*] You dregs, you emptied faces, have I shared my thoughts with you for nothing?

[*The dance of the masquerade becomes wilder, racked by spasms, the gradual build-up of possession.*]

SAY T.: Stop it! Stop it! [*Hitting his gang wildly.*] Who you calling boss anyway? I say stop playing along with this sacrilege.

PROF. [*with a terrifying roar.*]: Play!

SAY T.: This has gone far enough.

PROF.: You make yourself conspicuous. Sit down!

[*The egungun has become thoroughly possessed. Say T., seeing this leaps at Professor, neatly wrests the gourd from him and smashes it against the far wall.*

The figure is suddenly still. For some moments they both stand motionless, facing each other. Suddenly they lock. With no sound but hissed breaths they heave and gripe at each other in a tense elastic control.

Salubi watching intently, dips his hand in his pocket and brings out a clenched fist. Finding a moment when Say Tokyo is well placed, he slides an object along the bench and Professor, who has not looked at the combatants at all is attracted by this movement and leaps for his stick, too late. Say Tokyo grasps the knife as Professor's stick hits Salubi hard on the wrist, plunges the knife in Professor's back. Professor jerks upright, his face masked in pain. There is a dead stillness of several moments. Panicking suddenly, Say Tokyo attempts to pull the knife from Professor's back. The still mask appears to come to life suddenly, lifts Say Tokyo in a swift movement up above his head, the knife out and in Say Tokyo's hand, smashes him savagely on the bench. Say Tokyo

tries to rise, rolls over onto the ground and clutches the train of the mask to him.
Rising gradually, the driver's dirge.
Slowly the mask spins, spins, sinking lower as the Professor staggers to his table. He begins in an involuntary movement to gather up his papers. His strength falters. He makes a vague gesture of the hand, like a benediction.]

PROF.: Be even like the road itself. Flatten your bellies with the hunger of an unpropitious day, power your hands with the knowledge of death. In the heat of the afternoon when the sheen raises false forests and a watered haven, let the event first unravel before your eyes. Or in the dust when ghost lorries pass you by and your shouts your tears fall on deaf panels and the dust swallows them. Dip in the same basin as the man that makes his last journey and stir with one finger, wobbling reflections of two hands, two hands, but one face only. Breathe like the road. Be the road. Coil yourself in dreams, lay flat in treachery and deceit and at the moment of a trusting step, rear your head and strike the traveller in his confidence, swallow him whole or break him on the earth. Spread a broad sheet for death with the length and the time of the sun between you until the one face multiplies and the one shadow is cast by all the doomed. Breathe like the road, be even like the road itself.…
[*The mask still spinning, has continued to sink slowly until it appears to be nothing beyond a heap of cloth and raffia. Still upright in his chair, Professor's head falls forward. Welling fully from the darkness falling around him, the dirge.*]

GLOSSARY OF PIDGIN AND YORUBA WORDS

PIDGIN

3. dey — wey
   wey — which; who
   na — it's
4. still yet — even so; yet; still
   am — him, her, it
5. abi — or; 'do you mean to say'
   stiff — stiffen
   no — not; don't, didn't, wasn't it?
   fit — be able to
6. wes — what's the—?
   chop — eat
   Haba — ha !
   man wey — the man who
   chop life — enjoy life
7. jealous — envy (verb)
   fine fine — very pretty
14. Abi when etc.—Was he born with a steering wheel tied to his neck?
15. Why 'e no etc. — Why didn't he simply play the thing himself?
    Dat one no etc. — That's no church, it's high society.
17. for in — in his
    na so — just so (as I've described)
18. Politics no etc. — not even politics was as dramatic.
    Me a dey etc. — As for me I'm going to look for work.
    Where etc. — Where exactly are you running to?
       (self, kuku etc. serve as all sorts of emphasis)
25. no borer etc. — no borer in the old bole (my body is sound)
27. gorra — got to
29. Month ending na etc. — Month-end is time for settling debts.
    abi dis — or is this?
    wis, wes — which? what? what kind of?
    wetin — what

42. Tell Professor etc. — to remove his curse from my head.

43. doesn't to — doesn't; isn't; won't

59. All right etc. — All right I'm sorry I didn't know it was your child.

    God punish etc. — God punish you, you wretched woman, why do you lift your child the better to see such a thing? You think this a cowboy film? Get away my friend . . . . a-ah, these people are too foolish. Is this the kind of thing to show small children? If he has nightmares and begins to shout at night you'll then begin to panic. Foolish woman! Another man's calamity fulfils your entertainment.

64. . . . . you think this is a football game? Fai! fai! fai! You apply the brakes as if you are tackling a centre back. I say softly softly! . . . You can't walk but you want to fly.

82. Another time etc. — Another time the general sent a cablegram with his own hand. He said, award him Victoria Cross. I say give it him, black man or no black man—give him. They would have given me that but when the governor back home heard what they planned to do, he cabled back to say that if I was given that kind of superior medal, I would return to the country and become a political agitator. Ha! There is no justice in the white man's world.

    Lef' me etc. — Leave me! I say leave me. What business of mine is that? I don't care whether the Governor and his aide-de-camp finished the same hymn since yesterday. Did they fight in Burma? I thought this Rememberance Day was for our own countrymen who died in combat . . . Shut up yourself. I say shut up yourself. That is how we sang it in the army camp and if you don't like it get out of here; go chant Latin in a Roman Catholic church.

83. Wetin enh? etc. — What! What! You think I will not myself die some day? When a man dies, he's dead and that's the end of that. Please, if you see a motor accident do come and tell me. We understand good business . . . sell spare parts and second-hand clothes. What? You think I have time for sentimentality? I who have seen so many corpses that I cannot eat meat unless

it is overdone? Take yourself away my friend. Business is business. If you see an accident tell me and I'll run there before all these useless men clean out the place.

92. I'm all right. Ti o l'eru ese! — Light travellers only: no burdens of sin! Sweetheart . . . a-ah sweetheart, when a girl is as pretty as you only transports like ours will match her. What now sweetheart? Oh your suitcase? That's already inside. Of course. We are quick service, we are senior service . . . A-ah mama, do you mean you have to carry all this luggage on your head? Ah, there are no more gentlemen in this world. Come on ma'am we are moving off this moment, you are the very last passenger we can take . . . I say Kotonu, rev it up, rev it up vu-um vu-um . . . Mister, can't you hear, we are taking off this instant. Don't come delaying us. Service is first class, everything provided. If you want a piss we will stop. No delay! What's that you say? I said no delay. What traffic police? Do you know anything of this bus? No delay—no policeman will stop us on the road. This bus has six corners and we have left a bribe in each corner. No nonsense no trouble. Ah my good corporal, come and join our bus look at his neck plump and greasy; he has taken so much bribe that his neck is swollen like a pig's belly oh corporal do come on sir, come inside our bus . . . long time no see. Welcome sir, how is the family? Oh dear oh dear, you look so thin, thin as a sugar-cane. Too much work eh? Ah how sad, that's just the life of a poor policeman . . . bloody crook his tomato face is all shiny with bribe . . . Ah Mrs., Mrs., this is your very own bus waiting all this time for you . . .

YORUBA

18. ogiri-mouth — skunk mouth
25. Igi dongboro etc. — Nothing like a sound club on the back of a looney!

Yio ba etc. — May it land on your father.

Gbegi etc. — Wedded, not to a wife but to timber.

Yio ba 'ponri etc. — May it hit the fountainhead of your great grandmother.

Olomokuiya — Ah, what sufferings for such as give birth.

42. omo agbepo — son of the night scavenger
    ole n'gboro — Robber abroad, fearless one, will rob his own
      grandmother.
    iwin ogodo — imp of the swamp.

TRANSLATIONS OF YORUBA SONGS

19. (Drivers' dirge)

It's a long long road to heaven
It's a long road to heaven, Driver
Go easy a-ah go easy driver
It's a long long road to heaven
My Creator, be not harsh on me
Bandele's horse galloped home a winner
But the race eluded him.

20. (Drivers' dirge cont.)

This waist-ruff is piled high, high
This waist-ruff is piled high, the lady
Has made me wet my pants
Oh she is cause of my sticky pants
Some high ruff she's piled on her waist.
A harlot called me a eunuch, I rejoiced
In spite of that I will not take
A prostitute to wife
Oh they pile it high in Lagos
They really pile it high
In Lagos it was my eyes were opened,
It took Lagos to break the secret, where
An ancestral spirit turned mortal

28. (Thugs' war-chant)

Who meets Oro and makes no obeisance
What he shall experience!
When he's home he'll need a hot massage
What he shall experience!
When he's home he'll make thanksgivings
What he shall experience!

And if he fails to make home before dawn,
What he shall experience!
His skull shall tell the tales thereof—oh
What he shall experience!
Who meets Esu and fails to give way
What he shall experience!
Who struts arrogant before ancestral spirits
What he shall experience!

50. (Dirge for Kokol'ori)

It fogged suddenly at noonday
The sun asked, what is this wonder?
The dew of drought settled on my feet
Death deprives us of rain
The dew of drought settled on my breast
And the chill of fear took me
Death has sinned against us
A man among men is gone ... Kokol'ori

86. (Professor's praise-song)

Professor, our being like demon
Professor, our being like demon
The elder above us
The elder below
The hand that thinks to smash me, let it
 pause awhile
I have one behind me, coiled snake on Mysteries
He moults in season, coiled snake on Mysteries
The foe cannot pound the head of a Father's
 son like yam
Who holds discourse with spirits, who dines with
 the Ruler of Forests
He is the elder above us
He is our elder below ...